Satan and His Kingdom of Darkness

by Gordon Lindsay

Published by
Christ For The Nations Inc.
Dallas, Texas
P.O. Box 769000
Dallas, TX 75376-9000

Compilation and Revision 1998
All Rights Reserved

This book is a compilation and revision of several smaller books written by Gordon Lindsay. In this new edition, the New King James Version of the Bible is used unless otherwise noted.

TABLE OF CONTENTS

Part I: Satan's Rebellion and Fall

1   The Fall of Lucifer 11
     Lucifer's Original State
     The Cause of Lucifer's Fall
     Lucifer Corrupted by Personal Ambition
     The Rebellion of Lucifer
     Lucifer's Premise for Success in His Rebellion

2   Satan's Plan to Overthrow the Throne of God 17
     Lucifer's Seduction of the Angels
     The Near Success of Satan's Rebellion
     God Was Not Taken by Surprise

3   How Satan Planned to Continue His Rebellion 22
     Why Did God Delay His Punishment of Satan?
     God's Plan to Create the Human Race
     Satan's Plan to Continue His Rebellion

4   The Earth Became the New Theater of War 26
     The Creation of Adam and Eve
     Eve's Seduction by Satan
     The Fall of Adam and Eve
     Satan's Masterpiece: "You Will Be Like God" (Gen. 3:5)

5   Satan and Job 30
     The Challenge of Satan
     Job Becomes the Center of Conflict
     God Wins a Battle Through Job's Faithfulness

6   Satan — Ruler of This World 33
     Man's Dominion of This World
     Satan Usurped Dominion of the Earth
     Satan Usurped the Kingdoms of This World
     Satan Usurps the Worship of God
     Satan Usurps the Temples of God

Satan Establishes His Own Religions
Satan Will Produce His Own Messiah
Satan Exercises Control of the Elements

7   **Satan — The Father of Lies** 40
The Theory of Evolution and Satan's Fall

Part II: Fallen Angels and Demons

8   **Fallen Angels and Demons** 47
Fallen Angels Who Are "In Chains of Darkness"

9   **The Origin of Demons** 50
The Question of Origin
Satan Rules Through His Army of Demons
The Characteristics of Demons
Demons Are Personalities
Many Demons Can Occupy the Same Space

10   **Capabilities of Demons** 61
Demons Can Cause Deafness
Demons Can Cause Blindness
Demons Can Cause Infirmity
Demons Can Cause Jealousy
Demons Can Inspire Treachery
Demons Can Seduce
Demons Can Cause Insanity
Demons of the Sense Organs
Lying Spirits
Seducing Spirits
The Demon of Murder

11   **Stages of Demonic Control: Oppression, Obsession and Possession** 73
Demonic Oppression
Demonic Oppression of the Mind
Demonic Obsession
Demonic Possession of the Body

Demonic Possession of the Brain
Absolute Demonic Possession — Insanity
Exhibitionism — Sign of Demon Possession
The Final Fate of Demons

Part III: Demonic Manifestations and Delusions

12 Spirit Phenomena as Revealed in the Scriptures 91
The Magic of Egypt
Witchcraft — Spiritualistic Mediums

13 Case Studies of Delusions Caused by Seducing Spirits .. 95
Case I — The Deceiving Spirit
Case II — The "Unpardonable Sin" Delusion
Case III — Satanic Delusion of a False Religion
Case IV — The Deluded Evangelist
Case V — John Alexander Dowie's Seduction
Case VI — Peter Hurkos' "Special Gift"
Case VII — A Woman's Deliverance From Insanity
Case VIII — John Smith's Deliverance From Insanity
Case IX — The Danger of Trifling With Demons
Case X — The Demon-Possessed Intruder
Case XI — The Believers' Power Over the Enemy

14 Spiritualism 117
The Ouija Board
Spirit Photographs
Communication With the Dead
Materialization — Sorcery

15 Discerning Evil Spirits 125
Test I — Does the Evil Spirit Deny Any Part of the Word of God?
Test II — Does the Evil Spirit Deny Christ Has Come in the Flesh?
Test III — You Shall Know them By Their Fruits
Test IV — The Gift of Discernment

Part IV: Demons and the Occult

16   Sorcery and Divination 135
   Spirits of Divination
   Fortunetelling
   Psychometry
   Automatic Writing
   The Divining Rod
   Hypnotic Demons
   UFOs

17   Witchcraft: Black and White Magic 151
   Devil Worship
   Witchcraft in England

18   Witchcraft in Foreign Lands 156
   Idol Worship
   The Demons of Juju
   Voodoo
   The Firewalkers
   J.L. de Bruin Accepts a Challenge

19   The Demons of Spiritism 164
   The Case of the Witch of En Dor
   Spiritism and Haunted Houses
   Ghosts
   Reincarnation

20   Sorcerers of Yesterday and Today 177
   Jeane Dixon
   Arthur Ford
   Mrs. Tweedale's Psychic Powers
   Bishop Pike and the Seducing Spirits

Part V: Gaining Dominion Over Satan and His Cohorts

21   How Demons Gain Control 193
   The Story of King Saul
   Demons Are Not to be Trifled With

Casting Out Demons is a Practical Matter

22 Testing for the Presence of Evil Spirits **204**

Summary of the Habits of Demons

23 The Ministry of Casting Out Demons **211**

Devils Cast Out in the Name of Jesus
Casting Out of Demons Requires More Than Magic
Prayer and Fasting Needed to Cast Out Powerful Spirits
Binding the Demon
Can Demons be Cast Into the Pit?
Casting Out a Multitude of Demons

24 Christ Brings Deliverance to the Captives **221**

Christ's Dominion Over Satan Was
    Anticipatory of the Cross

Part I:

Satan's Rebellion and Fall

Chapter One

The Fall of Lucifer

The Bible states that in the beginning, Satan, then called Lucifer, was a sinless and righteous being. The record speaks of the original integrity and uprightness of the great archangel: "You *were* perfect in your ways from the day you were created, till iniquity was found in you" (Ezek. 28:15). This wicked creature, now the archenemy of God and man, was at one time a holy being and guardian of the throne of God. He was an object of divine confidence, an archangel entrusted with great authority. For a season, he discharged his duties faultlessly and in perfect obedience to God. He was far from being an adversary of God; his deeds and conduct were above suspicion, and he enjoyed the confidence of God to such an extent that the guardianship of heaven was entrusted into his hands. (Read Isaiah 14:12-15 and Ezekiel 28:1-19.)

Lucifer's Original State

The Scriptures describe in some detail the original state of this exalted being. He was son of the morning, the lightbearer of heaven. He possessed authority which, so far as we know, was only less than that of God Himself. As the "anointed cherub who covers" (Ezek. 28:14), he reigned as vice regent in God's holy mountain (biblical expression for Kingdom of God). "Wiser than Daniel" (Ezek. 28:3), there was no secret among the angelic hosts that was hidden from him.

Many Bible scholars believe that Isaiah 14 tells of the fall of Satan:

> How you are fallen from heaven, O Lucifer, son of the morning! *How* you are cut down to the ground, you who weakened the nations! For you have said in your heart: "I will ascend into heaven, I will exalt my throne above the stars of God; I will also sit on the mount of the congregation on the farthest sides of the north; I will ascend above the heights of the clouds, I will be like the Most High" (Isa. 14:12-14).

They also believe that Ezekiel 28 relates the cause of his fall — pride.

> Moreover the word of the LORD came to me, saying, "Son of man, take up a lamentation for the king of Tyre, and say to him, 'Thus says the Lord GOD: "You *were* the seal of perfection, full of wisdom and perfect in beauty. You were in Eden, the garden of God; every precious stone *was* your covering: the sardius, topaz, and diamond, beryl, onyx, and jasper, sapphire, turquoise, and emerald with gold. The workmanship of your timbrels and pipes was prepared for you on the day you were created. You *were* the anointed cherub who covers; I established you; you were on the holy mountain of God; you walked back and forth in the midst of fiery stones. You *were* perfect in your ways from the day you were created, till iniquity was found in you. By the abundance of your trading you became filled with violence within, and you sinned; therefore I cast you as a profane thing out of the mountain of God; and I destroyed you, O covering cherub, from the midst of the fiery stones. Your heart was lifted up because of your beauty; you corrupted your wisdom for the sake of your splendor; I cast you to the ground, I laid you before kings, that they might gaze at you"'" (Ezek. 28:11-17).

These passages indicate that during the primeval ages, Satan, also called Lucifer, was a holy being. He was apparently a powerful archangel possessing unusual wisdom who, at some time in the past, exercised great authority as vice regent of God's creation. Nevertheless, he was not satisfied with his exalted position, but in his heart aspired to a still higher place — one equal to God. This unholy ambition became sin to him, and eventually culminated in his open rebellion and expulsion from heaven. Some scholars believe that Revelation 12:4 indicates that one-third of the angels joined with him.

For reasons deemed wise by God, He did not immediately destroy Satan. Though ejected from heaven, Satan was permitted access to the lower heavenlies. Later in the Garden of Eden, he managed to seduce Eve and her husband into disregarding the divine prohibition of partaking of the fruit from the tree of the knowledge of good and evil. Thus they transferred their God-given dominion to Satan. For this reason, the devil holds a legal claim upon the earth during this age.

The Cause of Lucifer's Fall

How did this mighty archangel, Lucifer, son of the morning, fall from his exalted position into the depths of depravity to become the prince of darkness?

Lucifer was created the perfection of beauty. He possessed personality and charm that commanded the admiration of the host of heaven. It is not uncommon for those who are endowed with unusual beauty to acquire an inordinate desire for the admiration of others. Lucifer, although of angelic order, was no exception. Ezekiel 28:17 states, "Your heart was lifted up because of your beauty." The record indicates that in the course of events, Lucifer developed a strange self-infatuation. Little by little, he permitted the center of his universe to shift from God to himself. He would not have admitted it, yet in truth a change in his character was taking place of sinister and frightening portent.

Lucifer Corrupted by Personal Ambition

Lucifer possessed rare gifts. He had been endowed with great wisdom and knowledge, and to him were entrusted many of the secrets of creation. By reason of these unique gifts and abilities, God had exalted him to the position of vice regent over His creation. In this key position, with his wisdom and superior intelligence, Lucifer was enabled to have deep insight into the mysteries of the universe.

But there is a realm in which are involved the eternal purposes of God, which may be entered only through reverent faith and trust. He, as Creator, is the Judge of what is wise and right (Gen. 18:25). Lucifer, blinded by ambition, chose to question the wisdom of the divine will, and in so doing, committed his fateful and tragic error.

What was it in the will of God that had become distasteful to Lucifer? The reason is clear. We are expressly told that Satan sought to exalt his "throne above the stars of God," so as to be "like the Most High" (Isa. 14:13,14). But God in His eternal plan had reserved this exaltation, not for Lucifer, but for Christ. The right to sit down with the Father on His throne was given to Christ alone (Rev. 3:21). Lucifer, though vice regent, the chief archangel and the anointed cherub, was to hold a lesser position than Christ. When it became evident to Lucifer that he was not to have the supreme position, his ambitions were frustrated, which resulted in his rebellion. This passion for self-exaltation, this unbridled personal ambition, has caused many a man or woman to press heedlessly on in self-will to a fate similar to that of Lucifer's.

The Rebellion of Lucifer

Lucifer, up until this time, had discharged his duties blamelessly and without fault. There had been no reason for him to do otherwise. But now rebellion was birthed in his heart. Although God had given him everything but the throne, Lucifer was not satisfied. The dream of a universal kingdom, in which he wielded supreme power, stirred a restless ambition within him.

Apparently, he made no attempt to repress this unholy spirit of self-exaltation. The evil seed of pride was permitted to take root and continued to grow. In the end, it produced a harvest of misery and woe for himself and for those who followed him — only the Infinite may assess its full extent (I Tim. 3:6). The story of Lucifer's self-exaltation, rebellion and subsequent fall is briefly but clearly related in Isaiah 14:12-14.

Lucifer's Premise for Success in His Rebellion

A wicked being, especially one as calculating as Lucifer, does not commit a crime unless he sees some hope for success. How could this archangel expect to be successful in a venture which challenged the Creator for His throne? Possessing the knowledge that he did of God's divine omnipotence, how could he hope to be successful in a contest with the eternal will of Jehovah? The wicked of this world, in their foolish ignorance, may defy God; but the circumstances are not the same as in Lucifer's case. Infidels and atheists know nothing of God. On the contrary, Lucifer shared in the divine counsels and had knowledge of many of the Creator's secrets. He knew what he was doing.

It is certain that the devil's rebellion was not born from the impulse of the moment, but was the result of a coldly calculated and carefully thought-out plan. Though diabolical in character, it nevertheless proved in many respects to be strategically sound. We must concede that he had substantial reason to expect success. That Satan's plans were shrewdly laid is evidenced by the fact that his wicked conspiracy did succeed to an amazing degree. Far from being quickly subdued, this terrible rebellion has continued down to this present day — although assuredly, its days are numbered (Rev. 12:12).

The fact is that if God had not foreseen the entrance of evil in the universe and prepared a plan in advance to counteract it — a plan so secret that neither good angels nor the bad were aware of it

— the rebellion of Satan would have disrupted His whole program. But God, Who foresees all, had prepared for it. We shall look into this countermeasure that God had in reserve later. It is enough to say now that the plan was so amazing that it startled even the loyal angels.

Chapter Two

Satan's Plan to Overthrow the Throne of God

It is evident that Satan had reason to believe there was at least a possibility his plot would succeed, for otherwise he would hardly have attempted it.

We know that God had given Lucifer the power and authority as vice regent over His creation. It was his responsibility to guard the interests of God's Kingdom and to be on the alert against anything that might jeopardize its security. However, Lucifer betrayed the trust given him; therefore, he became God's archenemy of all time.

The extent of Lucifer's power in relation to even the most mighty of other heavenly beings is hinted at in Jude 9: Michael, the mighty archangel, when arguing with Satan over Moses' body, "dared not bring against him a reviling accusation, but said, 'The Lord rebuke you!'" This indicates that Lucifer's power was superior to that of all other created beings.

Nevertheless, the question remains: Did Lucifer believe that his power was sufficient to successfully conduct a rebellion against God Himself? The answer is found in a study of Scripture. God's plan was designed so that the administration of His government of the universe would be carried out by created beings. When Lucifer rebelled, though this event was the most crucial one in the history of the universe, God did not come down from His throne and personally engage him in battle. To have done so would have defeated His whole plan.

Scripture explains that the task of actual combat with Satan has been specifically delegated to created beings: "Michael and his angels fought with the dragon; and the dragon and his angels fought" (Rev. 12:7). So far as is revealed, God works in the created realm only through an agent — an angel, a human being, or Jesus Christ, the God-man, Himself.

Lucifer's act of rebellion did not diminish his power, except in the moral sense. He had been made custodian of the secrets of the universe, and now he proposed to employ this knowledge in a fearful conspiracy to dethrone God.

In Daniel 10, we are given an enlightening glimpse of the nature of the spiritual conflict that rages between the angels of God and those of Satan. This most revealing chapter discloses things that transpire in the unseen world. A high-ranking prince of Satan was actually able to withstand the angel of God for 21 days, during which time the angelic messenger was prevented from fulfilling an important mission delegated to him by God. Not until Michael, the archangel, came with reinforcements were the powers of darkness forced to withdraw from their prolonged and desperate effort to frustrate the divine decree (Dan. 10:12,13). This remarkable passage of Scripture teaches that only when there is a preponderance of force in favor of God's faithful angels, are the legions of Satan compelled to give way.

Likewise, when the powers of darkness instigated the betrayal of Christ hoping to destroy Him, Jesus declared that were He to pray to the Father for aid, angelic help would be dispatched to His rescue at once. Interestingly, because of the great concentration of evil forces coming against Jesus, it would have required more than 12 legions of angels to defeat the hostile power (Matt. 26:53). (Jesus did not request this help, however, but said to those who took Him, "This is your hour, and the power of darkness" [Lk. 22:53].) On the cross, Christ was accomplishing the moral defeat, rather than the physical defeat, of Satan (Jn. 12:31,32). The physical defeat of the devil is still to come.

It is evident that in Satan's original plan, he thought to secure the allegiance of the majority of the angels of heaven, and thus be in a position to overwhelm those who might persist in their loyalty to God. He would, therefore, deprive God of the means that He had designed for controlling and governing His creation. Satan could then proceed unhindered in the establishment of his own kingdom.

Lucifer's Seduction of the Angels

How did Lucifer hope to persuade the angels to join him in his rebellion? What glittering prize could he offer that would cause them to take such a fateful step? Perhaps we may fully understand the answer to this question only when we recognize that evil has an element of delusion in its nature (II Thes. 2:11,12). Evil is something with which even the wisest and most brilliant dare not play.

Jesus, in His statement concerning the defection of Satan, indicated that he deceived the angels. "He ... *does not* stand in the truth, because there is no truth in him. When he speaks a lie, he speaks from his own *resources*, for he is a liar and the father of it" (Jn. 8:44). The inference is that he lied to the angels at the time of his fall, as he later did to Eve.

Lucifer, believing his own lies, embraced the delusion that he had foreseen everything. He supposedly made provision for every contingency, and thought he could not fail. Even today, he and his fallen angels refuse to concede defeat, and they battle on in desperation, although the reality of their impending doom must be increasingly evident to them (Rev. 12:12).

We discover how Lucifer probably deceived the angels by studying how he deceived Eve. He denied the penalty of death that would be incurred if Eve disobeyed God. Eve, like one-third of the angels, allowed herself to be beguiled by Lucifer's words so that she was persuaded to take of the forbidden fruit. It was too late when she realized that she had been deceived. Eve and her husband were, therefore, thrust out of the Garden, "lest he put out his hand and take also of the tree of life, and eat, and live forever" (Gen. 3:22).

Eve was mortal and was in fear of death, but that deterrent was not sufficient to keep her (nor Adam, for that fact) from disobeying God's command. However, the angels were not restrained by fear of death. Unlike Adam and Eve, who were mortal, angels do not die (Lk. 20:36). Although Lucifer and his angels were thrust out of heaven after their rebellion, they nevertheless retained their power to continue their rebellion to this very day.

Moreover, previous to the fall of Lucifer and his angels, evil had never entered the universe, so far as we have record. The fearful results of sin had never been visualized by created beings — though undoubtedly, as with Adam and Eve, God had warned them of the consequences of disobedience. Nevertheless, they did not have a firsthand knowledge of sin's awful consequences. And like Eve, they did not have a deep enough faith in God to rely on the absolute integrity of His Word.

It is highly probable that Satan, in his seduction of the angels, followed the same course as he did with Eve. He undoubtedly painted a flowing prospect of the independence that would be theirs if they broke their allegiance to God — that in so doing they would become "like God," makers of their own destiny (Gen. 3:5).

Each angel was therefore thrust into a position of making a decision, just as every moral creature of the universe must at some time or another make a decision — a choice as to whether their allegiance will be to God or to self. In their moral reactions, humans are not too much different than angels. Both are affected by temptation. Both are free moral agents. In his present state, man is made "a little lower than the angels" (Psa. 8:5), but someday the redeemed are to be equal to the angels, and in some respects, exalted above them (Lk. 20:36; I Cor. 6:3).

The Near Success of Satan's Rebellion

The angels had to decide whether to remain faithful to the Creator or to follow Lucifer. One-third of the angels elected to follow Lucifer — an unspeakable tragedy. However, even so great a defection was not enough to insure the success of Satan's rebellion. Lucifer was not all-wise in his foresight of the future. When the count was taken, the number of those who had decided to join him in the rebellion was short of what he anticipated. He had miscalculated. Had he known the outcome, it is possible he would have changed his mind about leading in this act of treachery. The two-thirds of the angelic host that remained loyal to God rallied under the banner of the archangel, Michael, and ejected Lucifer and the insurgent angels from heaven.

God Was Not Taken By Surprise

We cannot imagine that God was taken by surprise by all this. He no doubt saw the wicked spirit of rebellion developing in Satan's heart, and it must have been indescribably grievous to Him. Yet apparently, having given angels a free will, there was nothing He could do to prevent Lucifer from rebelling. Lucifer knew what he was doing and preferred the gratification of self-will and self-exaltation to obedience to God. He will not coerce free moral agents, or they would cease to be such. They must be at liberty to make choices whether it be for good or bad. God's apparent failure to take notice of the gathering rebellion evidently encouraged Lucifer to continue plotting.

However, there was one thing God foreknew that the devil did not: the exact extent to which the rebellion would go. He knew it would terribly disrupt His Kingdom, but that it would not ultimately succeed. He foreknew Lucifer would be able to lure away less than a majority of the angels. And thus it proved to be.

Satan, however, had determined his fate. The rebellion, failing to achieve success in its initial phase, resulted in the devil and his angels being forced out of heaven. Now he was irrevocably committed to forever follow the course he had chosen.

Chapter Three

How Satan Planned to Continue His Rebellion

In planning his rebellion, did not Lucifer anticipate the possibility of failure? Evidently, he thought his chances of success were good enough to discount the possibility of failure. Even in failing to win over the majority of the angels to his cause, Lucifer did not consider that all would be lost. Though he had suffered a serious setback, he had reason to feel assured of the eventual success of his rebellion. And events were to prove that he was right — almost!

Lucifer's plan was a masterpiece of cunning and treachery. It was a betrayal that exploited to the fullest degree the great trust that God had reposed in him. How shrewdly his plans were laid is evidenced by the fact that the initial phase of his rebellion made a shocking inroad on the angelic population. No less than one-third of the heavenly host was persuaded to throw in their lot with him. That he secured so large a following reveals the magnitude of the rebellion as well as the widespread sympathy he had aroused for his cause. It is only too evident that he had been able to sow discord and dissatisfaction among the angels — probably by raising doubt concerning God's wisdom and goodness. This leads us to another question — one that has been a classic since the beginning of time.

Why Did God Delay His Punishment of Satan?

Why did God, after the devil rebelled, not punish him at once? Why did He permit him freedom to continue in his evil course? Though there is undoubtedly more than one reason, the one that stands out above others is that Satan, in seducing as many as one-third of the angels, must have succeeded in bringing into serious question the goodness and justice of God. For God to have a Kingdom that is enduring, He must execute justice in a manner which reflects His loving nature and fosters respect and reverence from the freewill agents He created.

In the case of Lucifer's rebellion, God considered it necessary to demonstrate how wicked, treacherous and disgraceful it was — to give humanity opportunity to observe how rebellion perverts holy beings into wicked and vicious creatures. Before executing the requisite punishment on Lucifer, God would first demonstrate the awful character of his act. He would give His subjects opportunity to witness the terrible consequences of sin.

In summary, God would justify the wisdom of His laws in the eyes of His creatures. Satan, essentially selfish, contended that no creature served God because he loved Him, but only for what could be gotten out of it.

God's Plan to Create the Human Race

After being ejected from heaven, Lucifer and his angels laid plans to continue the rebellion. The overall strategy was to abort the plan of God. Satan is not all-wise; therefore, he had to wait and see what steps God would take. Whichever way God should move, Satan planned to make a countermove.

God's next move soon became evident. The expulsion of Lucifer and his angels had left a void in the ranks of heaven. God cannot change from a course that He has chosen. "For I *am* the LORD, I do not change" (Mal. 3:6). God has a purpose for every creature He has created. If they fulfill that purpose, well and good. If they will not fulfill God's will, the divine purpose must still be accomplished.

For example, God chose Saul and his seed to reign over His people, Israel. But when Saul failed to carry out the divine plan, God raised up another king, David, to take his place (I Sam. 13:13,14). Although Lucifer and his angels refused to fulfill God's purpose in their creation, the Lord had no intention of permitting His purposes to be frustrated. He would raise up others who would take the place of those who rebelled. Although Lucifer had been made vice regent over God's creation, God proposed to create a new race to fulfill the purpose wherein the devil and his followers had failed.

Satan's Plan to Continue His Rebellion

As soon as Satan saw the unfolding of God's plan, he moved into action. He plotted to deceive this new race into following him instead of God. God also had something to prove: that He could find men and women who would stand true to Him, even under temptation and trial. Then He could shut Satan's mouth for all time. And to prevent the devil from having any further excuse, God gave him the opportunity to do the testing!

The devil lost no time in going to work. In the Garden of Eden, he tempted Eve. As we know, he succeeded in seducing her and her husband at the first try. He followed this success with another — he made a murderer out of their firstborn, Cain. It looked for a while as if Satan were winning the contest. Whole generations, yielding to his seductions, came under his sway.

However, there were some things that Satan had not foreseen. Despite his tremendous success, he was never able to corrupt *every* person belonging to a generation. There were always some who kept their faith in God. When whole generations fell away, there was still Enoch, who "walked with God" (Gen. 5:24). When the antediluvian world went into apostasy (Gen. 6:11), Noah obeyed God and prepared an ark to save his household (Gen. 7:1).

To his embarrassment, Satan discovered that there were always a few who would not yield to his seductions. Somehow God always succeeded in preserving a "righteous seed" on the face of the earth. This must have been extremely frustrating; success was so close, nearly within his grasp, yet it eluded him again and again.

However, there was something that always gave the devil confidence — man was now a fallen creature. Once the angels had fallen, they forfeited the prospect of ever returning into favor with God. What about man? Surely there was no way to be redeemed from their fallen condition.

Satan, essentially a selfish being, could not conceive and therefore anticipate, such a noble thing as God's plan of redemption: Christ divesting Himself of eternal glory, becoming flesh and dying in the sinner's place. Satan's lack of foresight in this respect would prove to be his undoing.

Chapter Four

The Earth Became the New Theater of War

Satan's strategy was to demonstrate that the human race would not serve God unless He gave them everything they wanted. If he could prove that, he would justify his own rebellion, and at the same time frustrate the plan of God. However, to be successful, he must alienate the whole race from God. There must be none left on His side to justify His wisdom and providence. Satan must corrupt the earth until there was no "righteous seed" left to transmit faith in God to a succeeding generation. If that happened, he knew God would have to destroy the earth's inhabitants.

Now it must be understood that God has never contended that all people would choose to serve Him. In making man a free agent, He gave him the power of choice, which implies the ability to choose against Him. But God *did contend* that there would always remain a "righteous remnant" who would serve Him, regardless of trial, temptation or suffering. In the end, there would be an aggregate of loyal people, even a "multitude which no one could number" (Rev. 7:9), who would follow Him wholeheartedly, and who would qualify for the place God had once intended for the angels that had rebelled. And so the drama of Satan versus man began.

The Creation of Adam and Eve

On the sixth day of creation, Adam and Eve were formed and placed in the Garden of Eden and given dominion over the earth (Gen. 1:26). The Garden of Eden was a beautiful paradise where every kind of tree abounded, including the tree of the knowledge of good and evil and the tree of life. The man and woman were given permission to eat of all the fruit of the Garden except the tree of the knowledge of good and evil.

The fact that God planted the tree of life in the midst of the Garden implies there was an important difference between this new race and the angels. Lucifer was not mortal, as is evidenced by the fact that he has been able to continue his wicked opposition to God through the ages with undiminished vigor. Man, however, was warned immediately after creation that the act of disobedience carried a penalty of death (Gen. 2:17). God was not giving physical immortality to any more creatures until they proved themselves worthy of the gift (Lk. 20:35,36; II Tim. 1:10).

However, it is evident that God intended for man to become immortal, for in the midst of the Garden, He had planted the tree of life — though apparently He did not immediately disclose its location to Adam. When man sinned, God decreed that he must leave the Garden, "lest he put out his hand and take also of the tree of life" (Gen. 3:22), and thus be able to live forever in his sinful state. In such an event, man might join forces with Satan, thus augmenting the rebellion against the Creator.

Eve's Seduction by Satan

Satan kept watch on the events that were taking place with a cunning eye. He was prepared, when the opportune moment arrived, to seduce the new occupants of the Garden of Eden to disobey the express command of God regarding partaking of the tree of the knowledge of good and evil.

Satan did not make his attack by direct onslaught, lest he drive the couple into the arms of their Protector instead of away from Him.

Satan took a bold step tempting the woman while Adam and Eve were together. Genesis 3:6 says, "She also gave (the fruit) to her husband with her." It did not take long for the evil nature of the temptation to be detected.

One day when Eve was in the Garden, Satan embodied himself in a serpent, which at the time was not the crawling, repulsive reptile we now know. It was only after the curse that it was degraded and cast upon its belly (Gen. 3:14). It is therefore inferred that the serpent previously stood upright and was probably the most intelligent and beautiful of the beasts of the field (Gen. 3:1).

Evil sometimes has a mysterious fascination. Instead of keeping away from the prohibited tree, apparently Eve's curiosity drew her toward it, where she stood musing over the strangeness of God's prohibition. It was while indulging in this foolish curiosity that the serpent appeared on the scene and engaged in conversation with her. Satan's plan was to confuse Eve, and by subtle suggestion, get her to transgress God's command by partaking of the forbidden fruit. It has been well said that Eve's first mistake was in going near the tree. Had she avoided the vicinity, she would never have cast the covetous glance upon it that resulted in her yielding to temptation and thereby bringing sorrow upon herself and her descendants.

The Fall of Adam and Eve

Eve listened to the subtle words of the deceiver. Beguiled by her unsuspected archenemy, she succumbed to his temptation. Eve took of the fruit, then persuaded her husband to share in her act of disobedience. "Adam was not deceived" (I Tim. 2:14), but he was foolish. He knew what the penalty was, but in a moment of panic, rather than lose the beautiful creature that God had given him, he decided to share her fate. That is how sin entered the world.

To all appearances, Satan had won an important and perhaps decisive round. He had deceived the first parents; therefore, the entire human race would be a fallen race. The devil's contention that man would not stand under temptation, received strong confirmation. Moreover, man's dominion over the earth had now been passed over to the devil as a consequence of disobedience (Lk. 4:5,6).

Satan's Masterpiece: "You Will be Like God" (Gen. 3:5)

It is interesting to note the order of Satan's temptation of Eve. First, doubt was cast on the integrity of God's Word and on His goodness: "Has God indeed said, 'You shall not eat of every tree of the garden'?" (Gen. 3:1). Why should God forbid Eve to partake of fruit that appeared so good for food? When Eve innocently answered the serpent that if she ate the fruit, death would result, the devil was ready for the next step in the temptation.

Was not the reason God forbade them to eat of the fruit that He knew they would become wise, knowing good and evil "like God"? As to the penalty of disobedience that Eve referred to, Satan boldly lied: "You will not surely die" (Gen. 3:4). By this time, Eve was in the serpent's trap. She reached forth her hand, and the irreparable deed was done.

Satan's subversion of the angels was not, of course, the same as that of Eve, but it seems likely that he had told them that they would become "like God" if they would follow him. Jesus said of Satan: "He was a murderer from the beginning, and *does not* stand in the truth, because there is no truth in him. When he speaks a lie, he speaks from his own *resources*, for he is a liar and the father of it" (Jn. 8:44).

Following the fall of Adam and Eve, the curse fell upon the serpent in which Satan had embodied himself to carry out the deception. God pronounced a curse upon the earth and a sentence of death upon Adam and Eve. All this fitted in well with Satan's plans. In that moment, "the power of death" passed to Satan.

Chapter Five

Satan and Job

To fully understand Satan's plan of action against humanity, we turn to the book of Job, which throws positive light upon God's reason for permitting Satan freedom to tempt humanity.

Significantly, the book of Job was probably the first book of the Bible to be written. It was obviously written before the Law, for it would scarcely have been possible to discuss the whole field of divine providence while avoiding reference to the Law if it had been known. In all probability, Job is the first written document of any kind. So we can see how vitally important the first chapters of Job must be since they are apparently God's first written words to man.

These chapters show how Satan, after being cast out of heaven, carried on his warfare against God. They also reveal the character of this war, which has now shifted its theater of action from the heavenlies to the earth.

The Challenge of Satan

In Job 1:6, we are told that on a certain day when the sons of God presented themselves before the Lord, Satan came also among them. The Lord took note of his presence saying, "From where do you come?" (Job 1:7). This statement reveals that Satan no longer dwelt with the righteous angels, since his presence among them was abnormal. It also tells us that though the fallen angels no longer dwelt with the loyal ones, Satan still had access to the presence of God.

The devil had one purpose in his visit: to call God's attention to how thoroughly evil had triumphed on the earth, thus supporting his contention that man would not serve God if the temptation was sufficiently strong to do otherwise.

Job Becomes the Center of Conflict

God answered Satan by reminding him of His servant, Job: *"There is none like him on the earth, a blameless and upright man, one who fears God and shuns evil"* (Job 1:8). He called Satan's attention to Job's integrity and faithfulness to Him. Satan had his stock answer ready. He accused Job of fearing God only because of what he could get out of it. He said that God had protected Job, made a hedge about him, and given him wealth and prosperity. Satan contended that if God failed to continue to shower blessings upon Job, he would turn against Him and curse Him to His face (Job 1:9-11).

Satan's belief was that every person was like himself — self-centered. In other words, he was telling God that men served Him only as a cold business proposition. Satan knew the only way for God to answer his indictment was to put man to a test. God accepted the challenge and permitted the test to take place.

With permission granted, Satan went forth to bring disaster upon Job. The Sabeans came and took away Job's oxen and donkeys. The Chaldeans stole his camels and massacred his servants. Then, as a crowning misfortune, his children were slain in a violent storm which destroyed the house of Job's oldest son, where they were having dinner together (which shows Satan's active role in a destructive storm).

But God's confidence in Job was not misplaced. The godly patriarch would not relinquish his faith in God: *"The LORD gave, and the LORD has taken away; blessed be the name of the LORD"* (Job 1:21). Poor Job. God could not reveal to him the true nature of the events that were taking place — that it was actually the Lord Who had given to Job, and the devil who had taken away. Nor could Job realize that he was the center of attention of two worlds — hell and heaven. God and His loyal angels and the devil and his fallen angels were all watching with intense interest to see the outcome of the test Job was going through: Although Job was humbled and broken, he stood true to God.

Again the devil came before God, and again God called his attention to Job, who had faithfully maintained his integrity, despite the fiery trials and the cruel sorrows he had endured — the loss of his property and children — at Satan's hand. But Satan was not yet silenced. His impudent answer was, "Skin for skin! Yes, all that a man has he will give for his life. But stretch out Your hand now, and touch his bone and his flesh, and he will surely curse You to Your face!" (Job 2:4,5).

It is evident that God, in granting Satan permission to put boils upon the flesh of Job, had an important purpose. God's contention was that regardless of how great the temptation or trial Satan might present, there would always be those who would serve God.

God Wins a Battle Through Job's Faithfulness

Satan went out from the presence of God and afflicted Job with boils from head to foot. Job's wife gave in to hopelessness and advised him to "Curse God and die!" (Job 2:9). Job indignantly rejected this suggestion and rebuked his wife for those impious words. His friends came and viewed his abject condition, but they could not explain the riddle of his misfortunes. They concluded that he had committed some grievous sin. Neither could Job account for his predicament; he believed that God had smitten him for inscrutable and mysterious reasons. He knew nothing of the dramatic character of the conflict that raged and was unaware that it was Satan who had placed the boils upon him.

Nevertheless, Job rose to sublime heights of faith when he said, "Though He slay me, yet will I trust Him" (Job 13:15). By those words, Satan's indictment that no human would serve God if the trials and temptations were great enough, was proven false. Job, by his faithfulness, justified God's confidence in him as well as vindicated the integrity and soundness of the plan of God. When the test was over, God healed Job and gave him twice as much as he had before (Job 42:12-17).

Chapter Six

Satan — Ruler of This World

Man's Dominion of This World

The fact that Satan now has control over the kingdoms of this world does not mean that God gave the control to him. The truth is that God originally delegated the dominion of the earth to man. "Then God said, 'Let Us make man in Our image, according to Our likeness; let them have dominion ... over all the earth.' ... Then God blessed them, and God said to them, 'Be fruitful and multiply; fill the earth and subdue it'" (Gen. 1:26,28).

Adam and Eve, therefore, obtained their authority directly from God, and the earth was theirs to rule — in harmony, of course, with the revealed will of God. "Adam was not deceived, but the woman being deceived, fell into transgression" (I Tim. 2:14). Adam became a traitor to God by relinquishing the dominion of the earth to God's great adversary, the devil (Rom. 6:16). Because of man's sin, the devil became the ruler of this world.

Jesus referred to Satan as "the ruler of this world" (Jn. 12:31; 14:30). The Apostle Paul speaks of him as "the god of this age" (II Cor. 4:4). The implication of these and other Scriptures is that Satan, during this age, largely dominates the affairs of our planet. We regretfully testify that this is only too true. This explains how men like Adolf Hitler and Joseph Stalin could commit monstrous crimes against humanity. Satan, in his role as "the ruler of this world," has usurped man's dominion, which the Creator intended to be beneficent.

Satan Usurped Dominion of the Earth

Satan's usurpation of dominion over the world is clearly shown in the temptation of Jesus. When the devil tempted Jesus, he took Him up to a high mountain and showed Him the kingdoms of this world. He made a curious and remarkable statement: "All this authority I will give You, and their glory; for *this* has been delivered to me, and I give it to whomever I wish" (Lk. 4:6).

It is true that the devil is a liar; however, the purpose of his lies is to deceive. Thus the devil must have been telling the truth to Jesus when he claimed that the kingdoms of this world had been delivered to him. For Jesus certainly would have known if he were not telling the truth, in which case it would have been no real temptation.

Satan Usurped the Kingdoms of This World

Satan's takeover of the kingdoms of the earth is a fact generally unrecognized by historians. Some deny the very existence of the devil, which only makes it easier for him to carry out his diabolical schemes.

To maintain his grip on the kingdoms of this world, the devil uses his own highly organized, invisible but real kingdom. While men and nations war against each other, the devil holds a strong hand on the evil spirits of his domain, requiring each of his emissaries to fulfill the tasks assigned without engaging in personal rivalries.

> But He (Jesus), knowing their thoughts, said to them: "Every kingdom divided against itself is brought to desolation, and a house *divided* against a house falls. If Satan also is divided against himself, how will his kingdom stand? Because you say I cast out demons by Beelzebub" (Lk. 11:17,18).

The subjects of Satan's kingdom are banded together in a common cause: to destroy the Kingdom of God. Each fallen angel or demon carries out its part in the war against mortals through deceiving and deluding them, by physically incapacitating, or even by taking their life before their time. Satan, within certain limitations, has the power of death (Heb. 2:14).

We must give the devil his due; he is a shrewd strategist. In prosecuting his rebellion against God, he concentrates his forces on objectives which he considers strategically important. This explains why so many consecrated saints of God at times go through bitter experiences of persecution and trial. Usually they do not realize that Satan has honored them by attacking them. The enemy is wise enough to perceive who it is that seriously threatens his interests.

Satan Usurps the Worship of God

When Satan tempted the Lord, he made a bid for His worship. Jesus, of course, rejected the offer and indignantly rebuked the devil for his blasphemous suggestion.

To a large degree, however, Satan has secured the worship of the human race. Hinduism, Buddhism, as well as spiritualism, etc. are examples of his success in recruiting people, either knowingly or unknowingly, to worship him. Idol worship as a rule is a direct worship of demons. Though the people worship idols, they generally recognize that there is a spirit entity behind them.

> Rather, that the things which the Gentiles sacrifice they sacrifice to demons and not to God, and I do not want you to have fellowship with demons (I Cor. 10:20).

In some countries of the world, the worship of evil powers is common. Many terrible and inhumane practices are performed to appease the "gods." In some pagan rituals, even children are sacrificed, violated or thrown to the river gods. Victims are whipped and flogged and even crucified to satisfy the frenzy of the demon's lust for blood. The devotees of these religions seem to obtain a sensual gratification while indulging in these depraved religious orgies.

Certain governments are now attempting to curb the more repulsive forms of such worship, but it still goes on.

Devil worship is a common thing in such lands as Tibet and Nepal. There have been well-documented stories of priests, who through chanting and worshiping the being they call the "king of hell," are able to actually materialize his diabolical form. Spiritualists find that they secure their most effective psychic response when they give worship to these spirits which are impersonating the dead. And not a few have entered into what practically amounts to a covenant with the devil.

The more extreme forms of devil worship do not normally occur in the United States, although spiritualism has gained a strong foothold. One thing is certain: Underneath it all is the fact, whether it is recognized or not, that man is a creature with an instinct to worship. If he does not worship God, he will worship something. If it is not a heathen image, it may be the god of money, the god of popularity or the god of sensuous gratification.

Satan Usurps the Temples of God

> Do you not know that your body is the temple of the Holy Spirit *who is* in you, whom you have from God, and you are not your own? (I Cor. 6:19).

It is God's plan that His Spirit should dwell in His people. The Apostle Paul declared that the Church is "built on the foundation of the apostles and prophets, Jesus Christ Himself being the chief corner*stone* ... in whom you also are being built together for a dwelling place of God in the Spirit" (Eph. 2:20,22).

God purposed that His Spirit should abide with the Christian forever (Jn. 14:16). If God is not permitted to inhabit the person, then the devil seeks to do so. This is what happened to Judas. After he made the decision to betray his Master, "Satan entered him" (Jn. 13:27). The devil does not personally enter people; this is reserved for his army of demons.

Usurping God's place by dwelling in the bodies of men, the

enemy is able to accomplish his evil purpose. As when Christ's Spirit dwells in people and they become like Him, bearing the fruit of the Spirit (Jn. 15:5), so when demon spirits dwell within a person, the individual's character coarsens, and he gradually takes on evil characteristics.

Satan Establishes His Own Religions

As ruler of this world, Satan has established many kinds of worship. Even under the name "Christian," all sorts of religions parade. They all have an appeal of their own. They usually have a certain fascination to the natural man and are not without some elements of truth; but in each case something vital is omitted. Denial of the deity of Christ and the efficacy of His blood are telltale marks of these pseudo-Christian religions.

> For certain men have crept in unnoticed, who long ago were marked out for this condemnation, ungodly men, who turn the grace of our God into lewdness and deny the only Lord God and our Lord Jesus Christ (Jude 4).

Peter calls attention to false teachers and their ultimate end:

> But there were also false prophets among the people, even as there will be false teachers among you, who will secretly bring in destructive heresies, even denying the Lord who bought them, *and* bring on themselves swift destruction (II Pet. 2:1).

As ruler of this world, Satan establishes his own forms of worship, ordains his own prophets and anoints them with his own spirit, and produces his own substitutes for the Bible (i.e., Koran, the "holy writings" of the East). All these, of course, are wretched and worthless substitutes for the pure Christian faith. The true Church has before it a tremendous task if it is to reach the peoples of the world with the whole Gospel in the short time that is left.

Satan Will Produce His Own Messiah

Satan's practice is to counterfeit God's plan. As Christ is the true Messiah, so Satan must have his false messiah. Jesus alludes to this when speaking to certain Jews who did not believe in Him.

> I have come in My Father's name, and you do not receive Me; if another comes in his own name, him you will receive (Jn. 5:43).

Paul speaks about this man of sin yet to appear in the world:

> And then the lawless one will be revealed, whom the Lord will consume with the breath of His mouth and destroy with the brightness of His coming. The coming of the *lawless one* is according to the working of Satan, with all power, signs, and lying wonders, and with all unrighteous deception among those who perish, because they did not receive the love of the truth, that they might be saved. And for this reason God will send them strong delusion, that they should believe the lie, that they all may be condemned who did not believe the truth but had pleasure in unrighteousness (II Thes. 2:8-12).

Apparently, even as God incarnated Christ and gave Him His authority (Jn. 3:13; 5:19), Satan will bring forth his Antichrist and give him such power and authority that men will worship him.

Satan Exercises Control of the Elements

As ruler of this world, Satan is also "the prince of the power of the air" (Eph. 2:2). Satan does not have absolute control; however, he does have power over many things. This is true in respect to the elements. Satan was evidently responsible for the lightning that struck Job's sheep and consumed them (Job 1:16). He was also responsible when the great wind came out of the wilderness and destroyed the house where Job's sons and daughters were eating and drinking (Job 1:18,19).

And the LORD said to Satan, "Behold, all that he has is in your power; only do not lay a hand on his *person.*" So Satan went out from the presence of the LORD (Job 1:12).

It is also likely that Satan had something to do with the storm which swept across the Sea of Galilee while Christ was asleep and caused the disciples to fear that they would perish. Of course they were quite mistaken. For no ship that was ever made could sink while Christ was in it! Jesus "arose and rebuked the winds and the sea, and there was a great calm" (Matt. 8:26). The fact that Jesus "rebuked" the elements indicates that He was addressing an intelligence behind the storm, rather than the impersonal elements which merely react to the laws of nature.

Chapter Seven

Satan —
The Father of Lies

The Theory of Evolution and Satan's Fall

In *The Twilight of Evolution*, Henry M. Morris introduces a most interesting explanation of the origin of the theory of evolution and associates it with the original fall of Satan. Although the explanation is novel, it has much in its favor. Mr. Morris points out that evolution did not attribute its origin to Charles Darwin. The doctrine of spontaneous generation was generally believed by the ancients. The idea of creation by an omnipotent God is almost unique and is found only by revelation of the holy Scriptures.

The evolutionary theory, in some form or another, has dominated secular thought. The question is then, how can we explain such a widespread belief in a theory that is so contrary to scientific evidence? The answer is found in II Corinthians 4:3,4:

> But even if our gospel is veiled, it is veiled to those who are perishing, whose minds the god of this age has blinded, who do not believe, lest the light of the gospel of the glory of Christ, who is the image of God, should shine on them.

Satan has blinded the minds of men so that they have sought some plausible explanation of the universe as an alternative to the biblical account of creation. If it could be proved that men evolved through the evolutionary processes of nature, then they would owe no allegiance to a Creator. They would not be of a fallen race, and would have no need for redemption.

Satan, being the father of lies, has originated this monstrous falsehood through the centuries. And as we analyze the matter, we see that the truth or falsity of the theory of evolution becomes the one and basic issue that mankind faces. It is the matter of whether or not God is the sovereign Ruler of the universe, and whether man does or does not owe Him absolute allegiance.

All religions, except Christianity, are more or less creature-centered. They all revolve around some system in which man may better himself, rather than submit himself to the grace of God by which alone is salvation obtained. This brings up the question of how Satan came to fall in the first place. Isaiah informs us that Satan rebelled against God by saying in his heart: "I will ascend into heaven, I will exalt my throne above the stars of God ... I will be like the Most High" (Isa. 14:13,14).

Why did Satan allow pride to enter his heart and deceive himself into believing that he could displace God from His throne? God had told him that he was a created being (Ezek. 28:13,15). Apparently, there came a time when he doubted this. The only evidence he had was that God had told him this was true. Mr. Morris follows Satan's reasoning:

> Could it not be that both he and God had come into existence in some way unknown, that it was just an accident of priority in time that enabled God to exercise control? With all his beauty and wisdom, Satan could undoubtedly win the allegiance of many other angels who had similar reason to question the word of God.
>
> But how could Satan possibly rationalize this notion that both he and God and all other beings had come into existence in similar fashion and, therefore, were essentially of the same order? If God had not created him, who

had? If God were not all-powerful, who was? In other words, who was really God? The only possible answer that could be given by Satan which could in any way rationalize his rebellion was that there was really no creator at all! Somehow, everything must have come about by a process of material growth, of development of evolution. If he would not believe the Word of God, then this is what he must believe.

And this is what he still believes! For despite the clear testimony of the Word of God concerning his ultimate defeat and eternal punishment (and Satan thoroughly knows the Scriptures), he still refuses to believe that it is really so. He continues to rebel and hope that he will ultimately be victorious in this conflict of the ages.

It is certainly possible that Satan's philosophy was what he essentially presented to Eve in the Garden. He implied that God's Word was not to be trusted, and that God was withholding knowledge from them which they had a right to have. If Eve would disobey Him by taking of the forbidden fruit, she would not die, but "be like God, knowing good and evil" (Gen. 3:5). Apparently, Satan's philosophy was that there were other gods besides God.

The drift of the antediluvian civilization was away from God to the exaltation of man as he makes his own destiny. The tragic apostasy of the human race is told in Romans 1:21,25: Men "became futile in their thoughts, and their foolish hearts were darkened. ... Who exchanged the truth of God for the lie, and worshiped and served the creature rather than the Creator, who is blessed forever. Amen."

In other words, evolution sees creation creating itself; therefore, there is no need of a Creator. Men resist the thought that they are morally accountable and that God will come in judgment someday. As the Apostle Peter said, "Scoffers will come in the last days, walking according to their own lusts, and saying, 'Where is the promise of His coming? For since the fathers fell asleep, all things continue as *they were* from the beginning of creation'" (II Pet. 3:3,4).

Therefore, it appears that all evil in the universe has had its genesis in some aspect of evolution, in which all things have come to be through the process of nature instead of through the direct creative act of God. It is the principle of man asserting his sovereignty against the sovereignty of God. Certainly, Mr. Henry Morris' argument is worthy of full consideration. If correct, it is a very clear explanation of why and how Satan fell.

Part II:

Fallen Angels and Demons

Chapter Eight

Fallen Angels and Demons

Fallen Angels Who Are "In Chains of Darkness"

Satan's angels apparently fall into two groups. One group includes those which are at liberty in the heavenlies assisting Satan in his war against the hosts of God. The other group is comprised of those whose freedom has been taken from them. These have been placed under "chains of darkness" to await the day of judgment.

> And the angels who did not keep their proper domain, but left their own abode, He has reserved in everlasting chains under darkness for the judgment of the great day (Jude 6).

This means that some of the fallen angels are no longer at liberty, but have been imprisoned in outer darkness. Having loved darkness rather than light, they have been given opportunity to taste of the everlasting darkness. The Apostle Peter declares that they have been cast down to hell to await judgment.

> For if God did not spare the angels who sinned, but cast *them* down to hell and delivered *them* into chains of darkness, to be reserved for judgment; and did not spare the ancient world, but saved Noah, *one of* eight *people,*

a preacher of righteousness, bringing in the flood on the world of the ungodly (II Pet. 2:4,5).

The word *hell* in this isolated case is neither translated from *Hades* (the abode of the dead) nor from *Gehenna*, a term used for the lake of fire. The word *hell* in this instance is translated from the Greek word, *tartarus*, evidently a prison house especially for fallen angels.

Why is it that certain of the fallen angels are at liberty, while others are bound "in chains of darkness" and denied their freedom? There are two possible answers to this question. Since the Apostle Peter mentions together in one sentence God's judgment on the earth through the Flood and the chaining of these angels, some believe that the two events are connected. Certain Bible scholars believe that "the sons of God" mentioned in Genesis 6:4 refer to the angels who "did not keep their proper domain" (Jude 6) and cohabited with "the daughters of men," producing a race of giants on the earth. They believe that as punishment, these angels were placed under chains of darkness. This is an interesting possibility, although open to some serious objections, such as the statement of Jesus that angels do not marry (Matt. 22:30).

Yet the Bible does say that some fallen angels are bound while others have retained their liberty. How do we account for this? Bear in mind that the Scriptures teach that there has been agelong warfare in the heavenlies. From time to time, certain principalities have been defeated and overthrown. For example, the prince of Persia was defeated by the archangel Michael. After this evil prince was stripped of his power and his kingdom brought to an end, was he left free to continue his activities, or was he made a prisoner?

While it is true that Satan has some kind of legal claim on the earth for a limited period, it also appears that his domain is gradually being overthrown. Many of his kingdoms have already fallen. Is it not possible that upon the defeat of these kingdoms prisoners have been taken? One thing is certain: Some fallen angels have been imprisoned, although the exact time they were apprehended is not known.

Certain fallen angels have apparently been bound and their activities curtailed, but it appears that at least some of them will be loosed for a little while during the closing days of the Great Tribulation when the judgments of God are released in the earth.

> Saying to the sixth angel who had the trumpet, "Release the four angels who are bound at the great river Euphrates." So the four angels, who had been prepared for the hour and day and month and year, were released to kill a third of mankind (Rev. 9:14,15).

It also appears that at the same time a great army of demons will also be loosed from the bottomless pit.

> Then the fifth angel sounded: And I saw a star fallen from heaven to the earth. To him was given the key to the bottomless pit. And he opened the bottomless pit, and smoke arose out of the pit like the smoke of a great furnace. So the sun and the air were darkened because of the smoke of the pit. Then out of the smoke locusts came upon the earth. ... Their faces *were* like the faces of men (Rev. 9:1-3,7).

However, the time of the activities of these evil powers is very short, being limited to five months (Rev. 9:10), after which they undoubtedly will be returned to the bottomless pit (Rev. 20:1-3). This brings us to the subject of demons.

Chapter Nine

The Origin of Demons

Demons are a class of fallen spirit beings of which the Bible takes frequent notice. They are called by various names: evil spirits, demons or devils. Although they are spirit beings, they are of a distinctly different order than either Satan or the fallen angels.

With the possible exception of Satan entering into Judas, we do not have record of fallen angels inhabiting human bodies. The fallen angels apparently have a spiritual body of some kind and do not have need of embodiment. Their sphere of activity is in the heavenlies rather than upon earth — although it is true that they will be forced out of the heavenlies during the Great Tribulation (Rev. 12:12).

Demons, on the other hand, eagerly seek human habitation. All evidence points to the fact that they are disembodied spirits, and therefore desire embodiment. Although demons are subordinate to the fallen angels, their activities are in harmony with the objectives and purposes of Satan. They play an important role in the devil's program.

The Question of Origin

Where did demons come from? This question has often been raised, and it is not easily answered. That demons, or unclean spirits, exist there is no doubt. But how they originated and fell is not fully clear, although enough is revealed in the Bible to give us a fair idea.

The Origin of Demons

While it seems evident that the demons are not to be included among the fallen angels which were cast out of heaven at the time of Satan's rebellion, it seems probable that their fall was in some way associated with this rebellion. Angels, not having physical bodies, do not die in the sense that men die (Lk. 20:35,36), although angels can sin and suffer spiritual death — separation from God.

Another important argument against fallen angels being demons is the fact that the latter have their habitat upon earth, while the fallen angels apparently occupy the heavenlies and are generally engaged in conflict with the angelic hosts of God (Dan. 10). This warfare in the heavenlies is graphically described by Paul in Ephesians 6:12, which we have quoted previously.

The saints who sit in heavenly places with Christ Jesus (Eph. 2:6) also participate in this warfare and are urged to put on the whole armor of God in order to stand against the evil day. Of course it is possible for Satan or one of his angels to enter temporarily into a human being (Lk. 22:3), but since they have access to the heavenlies, it would appear, all things considered, that they would not confine themselves to human bodies.

There is another theory held by some that demons are disembodied spirits of the progeny of angels and the "daughters of men" spoken of in Genesis 6:2. However, Jesus said that angels neither marry nor are given in marriage, and it seems unlikely that the "sons of God" spoken of in that chapter were actually angels. It certainly would be a most unusual prodigy for an angelic incursion of this nature upon the earth.

Such are the main views on the various origins of demons. The subject has a fascination, but fortunately the complete resolution of the problem is not necessary to an adequate understanding of the activities of demons, their habits and methods of operation. And it is this which is really important to understand.

Where demons originated we cannot be certain. However, vast numbers of them do exist, and they eagerly seek embodiment in human beings. There are those who believe that demons are actually the fallen angels who defected at the time of Lucifer's fall. That demons are not the same as fallen angels would seem evidenced by the fact that they are seeking embodiment. A demon finds rest only when it can secure habitation in a human body. Once it takes possession, it will remain there until it is forcibly ejected, or until the person's death (Lk. 11:15-26). It will never leave of its own accord.

Although the Bible is skimpy in its account of the origin of demons, we are given considerable information concerning their present habits and activities. In Luke 11:24-26, Jesus makes a most interesting statement concerning the eagerness of demons to inhabit the human body, and what demons do in the event they are ejected from their habitation.

> When an unclean spirit goes out of a man, he goes through dry places, seeking rest; and finding none, he says, "I will return to my house from which I came." And when he comes, he finds *it* swept and put in order. Then he goes and takes with *him* seven other spirits more wicked than himself, and they enter and dwell there; and the last *state* of that man is worse than the first (Lk. 11:24-26).

We also know that a demon must respect the power of the Name of Jesus. In the Great Commission, Christ said, "In My name they will cast out demons" (Mk. 16:17). He also spoke of the power He gave His disciples over demons when the Seventy returned, rejoicing because the demons had fled at their command.

> Then the seventy returned with joy, saying, "Lord, even the demons are subject to us in Your name." And He said to them, "I saw Satan fall like lightning from heaven. Behold, I give you the authority to trample on serpents and scorpions, and over all the power of the enemy, and nothing shall by any means hurt you. Nevertheless do not rejoice in this, that the spirits are subject to you, but rather rejoice because your names are written in heaven" (Lk. 10:17-20).

Referring again to the words of Jesus in Luke 11:24, we see that when a demon is cast out, he is unable to find rest and will seek entrance into another human body. If he finds this difficult to do, he may try to re-enter the body of the person from whom he was cast out. In the case mentioned by Christ, the demon returns and finds the house "swept and put in order." Upon this discovery, he takes with him seven spirits more wicked than himself and they enter in "and the last *state* of that man is worse than the first." The obvious lesson is: Demons have no right to dwell in the individual who professes the Name of Christ. However, if a person who has been freed from demon possession does not profess Jesus as Lord of his life, the demon then has a right to return and take possession of the person.

In the story of the maniac of Gadara, the man was possessed of a legion of devils — perhaps several thousand (Mk. 5:9). This shows that the laws which govern a physical body are not the same as those which govern a spirit. In the natural, two objects cannot occupy the same space. In the spirit world, as many as several thousand demons may occupy the same person.

John the apostle describes the world as being subject to the devil's wicked system. "We know that we are of God, and the whole world lies *under the sway of* the wicked one" (I Jn. 5:19). Satan apparently seeks to establish for his kingdom strategic centers of wickedness on the earth. Thus the people of Pergamos were said to dwell "where Satan's throne *is*" (Rev. 2:13).

The educational, social and political systems of the world do not recognize Satan's position of power. The intelligentsia of our day do not acknowledge the existence of a personal devil. They consider the phenomena of the spirit world as being entirely psychic, explainable in terms of the natural operations of the human mind. Thus they are blinded and deceived by the very powers which they deny exist.

Satan Rules Through His Army of Demons

One of the most vivid pictures afforded by the Scriptures of Satan's rule over the nations is found in Daniel 10. Here we are told of a certain prince of Persia withstanding the very angels of God. The term "prince of Persia" could not refer to the visible king of that nation, who would certainly have no power to war against an angelic being, but to the invisible prince in the army of Satan who resided in the heavenlies and exercised the real power over the kingdom of Persia.

This indicates that each nation may have an unseen, though very real, prince from the kingdom of darkness. Under the hegemony of these powerful fallen archangels of the spirit world, a multitude of lesser spirits operate and as far as possible, carry out the wishes of their supreme master — Lucifer. By means of the myriads of evil spirits, the devil is able to make his power felt in every part of the world.

Demons operate in diverse ways. They first seek to clothe themselves with human bodies, and then to deceive their victims and lead them into the deepest depths of delusion. All of them can be generally classified as lying spirits, for they deceive and delude the nations into rebellion against the true God. No demon may depart from the principles upon which this satanic kingdom is based, although the manner of their operations and deceptions varies greatly.

Jesus declared, "If I cast out demons by the Spirit of God, surely the kingdom of God has come upon you" (Matt. 12:28). Satan, therefore, is not unlimited in his power, and his plans may be thwarted and brought to nought through prayer and intercession. Daniel waited in prayer and fasting for three weeks before Michael the archangel was finally dispatched to render assistance to the angel who was contending against the prince of Persia. The result was a great victory, and the angel was able to get through to Daniel and inform him of the things he was desirous to learn about the future of his nation.

Daniel, through his prayers, played a vital part in defeating the hosts of darkness, and for his faithfulness he received the special commendation of the angel. The Scripture text is illuminating:

> And he said to me, "O Daniel, man greatly beloved,

understand the words that I speak to you, and stand upright, for I have now been sent to you." While he was speaking this word to me, I stood trembling. Then he said to me, "Do not fear, Daniel, for from the first day that you set your heart to understand, and to humble yourself before your God, your words were heard; and I have come because of your words. But the prince of the kingdom of Persia withstood me twenty-one days; and behold, Michael, one of the chief princes, came to help me, for I had been left alone there with the kings of Persia" (Dan. 10:11-13).

That believers' prayers play an important part in the warfare in the heavenlies is made very clear in Ephesians:

For we do not wrestle against flesh and blood, but against principalities, against powers, against the rulers of the darkness of this age, against spiritual *hosts* of wickedness in the heavenly *places*. ... Praying always with all prayer and supplication in the Spirit, being watchful to this end with all perseverance and supplication for all the saints (6:12,18).

Our warfare is not against flesh and blood but against the unseen spiritual powers of wickedness in the heavenlies that influence the actions of men to evil. The reason that the people of God must develop a strong prayer life is to ward off the attacks of these malicious spirits and render them powerless to carry out their evil designs.

During the Great Tribulation, Satan and his angels will be cast out of the heavenlies as the result of the warfare of the righteous angels and the prayers of the saints of God.

And war broke out in heaven: Michael and his angels fought with the dragon; and the dragon and his angels fought, but they did not prevail, nor was a place found for them in heaven any longer. So the great dragon was cast out, that serpent of old, called the Devil and Satan, who deceives the whole world; he was cast to the earth, and his angels were cast out with him. Then I heard a loud voice saying in heaven, "Now salvation, and strength, and the kingdom of our God, and the power of His Christ have come, for the accuser of our brethren, who accused them before our God day and night, has been cast down. And they overcame him by the blood of the Lamb and by the word of their testimony, and they did not love their lives to the death. Therefore rejoice, O heavens, and you who dwell in them! Woe to the inhabitants of the earth and the sea! For the devil has come down to you, having great wrath, because he knows that he has a short time" (Rev. 12:7-12).

Satan's being cast down to earth precipitates the fearful reign of the Antichrist. His reign is short, however, and at the appointed time, Satan and his hosts will be rounded up and cast into the bottomless pit.

The Characteristics of Demons

Demons are as different in their individual capacities, their habits, their ways, as human beings are — with this exception: Their objective is consistently malevolent, and they invariably seek the ruin of the souls of those whom they seduce and deceive.

Certain demons are specifically adapted to afflict the bodies of people. Others direct their operations toward deception and delusion. Some demons can be cast out readily, while others are so tenacious that they can be exorcised only by prayer and fasting. The Bible enumerates many kinds of demons.

When these spirits were created, they were holy beings. God does not create wicked spirits. God said of Lucifer before he fell, "You *were* perfect in your ways from the day you were created, till iniquity was found in you" (Ezek. 28:15). But Lucifer, becoming filled with pride, apostatized and came under judgment. The demons were apparently involved in his rebellion.

Perhaps at this point, God disembodied them. As human beings vary in their talents, abilities and powers, so these spirits, even after their disembodiment, retained the special aptitudes and capabilities of their former existence, although they turned to evil purposes. Some demons are more subtle than others in their operations and their capacity to deceive. Others, like the epileptic spirit, have much greater power. Once this kind of spirit gains control, it is able to resist expulsion more than others.

Seducing spirits engage in enticing men and women into immorality. Murderous spirits incite men to commit homicide or self-destruction. Familiar spirits enter into a sort of covenant relationship with a medium, pretending to be spirits of dead persons.

Demons Are Personalities

That demons are more than an evil influence but are actually personalities is proved in various ways, including their power of speech. Spiritist mediums in a trance are often unconscious of what the impersonating spirit is saying, and yet a very intelligent though delusive conversation may be carried on with them. These demons pretend to be the spirits of the dead, which is, of course, not so. They are evil spirits under the dominance of Satan. And though they operate in different manners, their ultimate purpose is to deceive people and lead them into darkness.

The writer has had varied experiences in which a demon has spoken. Ordinarily it seeks to hide its identity, but when exposed, it may speak in vicious and hateful language. Nell Hibbard in her book *Demonology* tells of an instance in which she dealt with a demon-possessed woman. We take the liberty to quote from it in this account:

> Several years ago, a frantic husband and some friends brought a poor demon-possessed woman from Fort Worth to our church for prayer. She was lying on her back in the nursery of the church when we arrived. As

we entered the room, the devils screamed through the woman's lips. Her eyes crossed and stood out as though they were on stems. Her face became so distorted that it lost a human resemblance. The right corner of her mouth drew underneath the center of her chin. White froth rolled from her mouth and stood an inch high like solid anchored banks.

"I hate you," a fiendish voice screamed, and the woman lunged toward me like an angry wild animal seeking her prey. As we pleaded the blood of Christ, instantly she stood dead still in her tracks as though someone had suddenly stopped her. Then the devil through her lips told me my sermon topic of the previous evening. Bear in mind that I was in Dallas, and the woman in Forth Worth, yet the devil knew that I had preached on demonology Sunday evening.

One imp snarled, "You tried to wreck our kingdom last night by telling the people the way we work and by telling the tactics we use. Well, you did give us a bit of trouble, but there's enough of us in here to give you and several others plenty of trouble." My blood momentarily chilled, but we began earnestly praying. For three days and two nights someone stayed with her in earnest travail before God. At the end of the second night, the last demon was cast out and she was gloriously liberated. That was an example of real demon possession. In that case, the demons not only possessed her, but controlled her physical body.

In a case I personally witnessed in my youth, the demon at first pretended to be the Spirit of God and warned us not to doubt. It had many things to tell us about the spirit world of heaven and hell, and it seemed to us at first to be genuine. But the Bible warns us to test the spirits (I Jn. 4:1-3), and in this case the spirit did not stand the test. When finally the evil spirit's identity was clear, it readily admitted it was a demon. The individual through whom the spirit had spoken had quite a battle, but was finally delivered from its power.

Many Demons Can Occupy the Same Space

It is a law of physics that only a certain amount of matter can occupy the same space at the same time. An enormous amount of pressure can be applied to a substance, water for example, and still it will not compress, or only a very small amount. Atomic scientists tell us that there has to be a total disruption of the atom before there can be a collapse of matter.

That's true in the physical universe. But what is true of the physical world is not necessarily true in the spiritual realm. With evil spirits, one or many can inhabit the same person; that is, fill the same space. When the Holy Spirit comes upon a person, He in no way diminishes the person's personality or spirit, but instead the person's whole being is quickened and made more alive. But an evil spirit, instead of blessing, acts like a malignant disease which not only injures but degenerates the whole person, body, soul and spirit. The more of these evil spirits that enter the person, the more powerful their control, and the more rapid the deterioration of the personality.

In the case of the man Jesus delivered from a dumb spirit, He afterward gave a solemn warning (Lk. 11:24-26). He said that the man must now fill his life with the things of God or else the evil spirit would return with seven more spirits. Thus the man's condition would be much worse than it was in the beginning.

There was Mary Magdalene, "out of whom had come seven demons" (Lk. 8:2). Obviously she was a hard case before deliverance, but afterwards she showed extreme gratitude for her deliverance, and disregarding any possible danger to herself was among the first to visit the tomb where Jesus was buried. The Lord, recognizing her great devotion, appeared to her first after He was risen (Mk. 16:1,9).

Seven or eight demons in one person seems a large number.

However, there have been individuals possessed of dozens and even scores of demons. In some instances, these have come out one at a time, calling their names as they left. Spiritist mediums who consort with these demons are blind to their satanic nature and mistake them for spirits of the dead.

It is not surprising that there is a system and order in the spirit world (Matt. 12:25,26). In spiritist séances, it is usual for a particular demon (who generally pretends to be a previous resident of the earth) to assume authority under the guise of a "guide." Other demons who wish to communicate with some client of the medium must do so through this guide. An important point to be remembered is that many evil spirits can converse, communicate and live together in the body of the same person, causing him misery and suffering.

The almost limitless capacity of the human body to be possessed of demons was well demonstrated in the case of a demoniac Jesus encountered. Before He delivered the lunatic, Jesus questioned the demons as to their names. The leader replied, "My name *is* Legion; for we are many" (Mk. 5:9). Now a legion in the Roman army was about 6,000 soldiers. This does not necessarily mean that the man was possessed by exactly 6,000 demons, but it does indicate there was a vast number; when exorcised from their victim, they violently disturbed 2,000 swine, insomuch that they stampeded into the sea and drowned (Mk. 5:13).

This indicates that a large concentration of evil spirits may generate enough demonic energy to create convulsions among living creatures, whether man or beast. This no doubt is a clue to the frenzied actions of an excited mob which sometimes commits incredible acts of violence. In saner moments, the same individuals would probably recoil at the very thought of such acts.

Chapter Ten

Capabilities of Demons

In the same way that the talents and abilities of human beings vary greatly, so evil spirits' capacities to do evil are diverse. Some may be cast out readily. Others are so stubborn and tenacious that they can be cast out only by prayer and fasting (Mk. 9:29). The Bible speaks of many kinds of evil spirits. Evil spirits can cause physical maladies such as blindness, deafness, epileptic seizures, etc. They can also deceive, seduce, make jealous, bring insanity, and so forth. We will take note of some of the habits and methods employed by these evil creatures.

Demons Can Cause Deafness

Demons are able to take possession of certain organs of the body by oppressing or settling on various nerve centers of the body. Thus auditory nerves, optic nerves, throat nerves, and the nervous system of the spine are all regions of attack.

When a spirit settles on the auditory nerve in the ear, it becomes paralyzed and ceases to function. Sometimes a spirit controls the auditory nerves of both ears, and the person goes completely deaf. On occasion, the evil spirit may paralyze not only the nerves of the ears, but those of the throat, so that the person is neither to hear, nor to speak. This, however, is not the problem in the majority of hearing-impaired persons who are mute only because they cannot hear. These people often can be taught to speak, although their words are spoken in a dull monotone. That is no doubt the case of the deaf man mentioned in the seventh chapter of Mark: "Then they brought to Him one who was deaf and had an impediment in his speech, and they begged Him to put His hand on him" (vs. 32). Jesus took him aside from the multitude and healed him, and he was able to both hear and speak (vs. 33-35).

When the body, soul and spirit are in healthy condition, they can resist the intrusion of an evil spirit. Sickness or an accident can weaken this natural resistance, making it possible for a demon to find entrance.

Demons Can Cause Blindness

It seems strange to some people that demons can cause blindness. Matthew 12:22 clearly shows it is so:

> Then one was brought to Him who was demon-possessed, blind and mute; and He healed him, so that the blind and mute man both spoke and saw.

There are cases in which an evil spirit resides on the optic nerves, paralyzes them and makes it impossible for the person to see. Usually, no amount of surgery can help the person who is thus afflicted. Of course, there are many diseases of the eye which are not caused by evil spirits. The eye is a very complex organ, and sight may be lost through a number of causes.

Demons Can Cause Infirmity

Evil spirits can control the body in various ways. One is by settling on the spinal cord, often resulting in the person's being twisted or bowed over, sometimes in a grotesque manner. Luke 13:11 tells of a woman who had an evil spirit, who "was bent over and could in no way raise *herself* up."

It is interesting to note that Jesus said that this woman was a daughter of Abraham, indicating that she was Abraham's child, not only by natural seed but by faith (Gal. 3:26,29). In other words, she was a believer. This shows that believers can be subject to infirm spirits. It should be noted that in all such cases, the devil is afflicting the body, not the soul. Actually, the devil has no right to afflict the body of a believer any more than his soul; if a person understands God's promises in this respect, he will not tolerate the enemy's oppression. It is up to Christians to recognize their authority and take dominion over evil spirits.

Demons Can Cause Jealousy

Certain spirits oppress the mental faculties and cause a noticeable deterioration in the person's spiritual life. Once a demon or demons obtain such control, the individual becomes progressively more jealous, suspicious and antisocial. There is often a marked change of personality.

Saul is a case in point. Saul started well, but did not seem to understand the importance of obedience. He did not fully carry out God's instructions. When Saul saw that his disobedience had caused him to lose favor with God, instead of repenting, he became suspicious of all others who seemed to threaten his position as king.

Brooding over his self-imposed misfortunes, the king developed an antipathy toward David to the point he was ready to kill him. And that was the opening for a jealous spirit to take possession of him.

By rejecting God's will and substituting his own, Saul no longer had the right to divine protection, and he became vulnerable to the attack of evil spirits.

> So Saul eyed David from that day forward. And it happened on the next day that the distressing spirit from God came upon Saul, and he prophesied inside the house. So David played *music* with his hand, as at other times; but *there was* a spear in Saul's hand (I Sam. 18:9,10).

Demons Can Inspire Treachery

Abimelech, who usurped the throne of Israel and made himself king in the days of the judges, was another example of how a man by his conduct can come under the power of treacherous and murderous spirits. Abimelech committed an infamous act of mass murder: the slaughter of 70 of his brothers, sons of Gideon. Because of this, God permitted an evil spirit to incite rebellion among the men of Shechem.

> After Abimelech had reigned over Israel three years, God sent a spirit of ill will between Abimelech and the men of Shechem; and the men of Shechem dealt treacherously with Abimelech (Judg. 9:22,23).

The result of the uprising against Abimelech was civil war that terminated with his death.

Demons Can Seduce

There are religious demons who apparently have special talents for luring people into false religions. These spirits give false revelations and teach unscriptural doctrine to persons lacking humility and possessed with inordinate personal ambition. The Scriptures declare that this will especially be the case in the last days. The false religions that are arising on every hand bear witness to the accuracy of this prophecy:

> Now the Spirit expressly says that in latter times some will depart from the faith, giving heed to deceiving spirits and doctrines of demons (I Tim. 4:1).

These false spirits profess to give "new revelations" which have a superficial plausibility, but are actually at gross variance with the Word of God. Such "revelations" almost invariably play to the person's ego or pride by making him believe he is better than others.

Demons Can Cause Insanity

These demons are usually spoken of in Scripture as "unclean spirits." They may take possession of a person and drive him completely out of his mind and in some cases, making him a raving maniac. While Christ was ministering in the synagogue at Capernaum, an unclean spirit cried out: "Let *us* alone! What have we to do with You, Jesus of Nazareth? Did You come to destroy us? I know who You are — the Holy One of God!" (Mk. 1:24). Christ cast out the evil spirit and set the man free, to the amazement of the onlookers.

There is a much more violent instance — the man possessed of a legion of devils in Mark 5:1-19. The demons tormented his body so that he ran from the presence of men and lived among the tombs. Many times his hands and feet had been chained, but the power of the demons was so great that he was able to break the chains every time. He was so strong that no one could control him. "And always, night and day, he was in the mountains and in the tombs, crying out and cutting himself with stones" (Mk. 5:5). Jesus cast out the evil spirits, and the man was made whole.

There are also spirits which possess mediums and impersonate the dead, which we shall deal with more fully later.

Demons of the Sense Organs

Certain demons are able to assume a measure of control over a person's physical body through the major nerve centers of the sense organs. It should be noted that these kinds of spirits do not necessarily acquire dominion over the moral nature of the person. But they are often able to afflict devoted Christians who do not understand their authority over Satan.

It should be understood that not all afflictions are directly caused by demons. Most diseases are caused by virus or various kinds of germs or bacteria. However in many cases, such diseases weaken the body so that an infirm spirit may get control of some organ of the body. To secure complete deliverance the afflicting spirit must be cast out. Thus Peter's mother-in-law was ill with a great fever, which perhaps began with a virus. But Jesus recognized that an afflicting spirit of some kind was there and had taken advantage of the condition and was oppressing the woman. He, therefore, rebuked it, resulting in the mother-in-law's immediate deliverance.

Lying Spirits

Then *Micaiah* said, "Therefore hear the word of the LORD: I saw the LORD sitting on His throne, and all the host of heaven standing by, on His right hand and on His left. And the LORD said, 'Who will persuade Ahab to go up, that he may fall at Ramoth Gilead?' So one spoke in this manner, and another spoke in that manner. Then a spirit came forward and stood before the LORD, and said, 'I will persuade him.' The LORD said to him, 'In what way?' So he said, 'I will go out and be a lying spirit in the mouth of all his prophets.' And He said, 'You shall persuade *him*, and also prevail. Go out and do so'" (I Ki. 22:19-22).

This incident throws light on the activities of demons in the spirit world. King Ahab had persuaded the godly Jehoshaphat to join him in a military venture to take Ramoth Gilead. King Ahab was married to the wicked Jezebel, a woman utterly void of principle. Ahab's first step was to consult his oracles. Ahab's prophets were instructed to prophesy good things. So all of Ahab's prophets prophesied certain victory. Scriptures reveal that these prophets were possessed by lying spirits. Naturally, deceiving spirits do not always lie. Their powers of deception depend on their telling the truth until they have gained the confidence of their victims.

It is interesting to recall that Adolf Hitler was in the habit of consulting seers and astrologers. His oracles, time after time, prophesied victories which came to pass so consistently until all Europe was believing Hitler was invincible, that he was born under a lucky star. Attempts were made to assassinate him, but apparently he lived a charmed life. It was after Hitler was convinced that he was infallible that "stars from their courses fought against" him (Judg. 5:20). At a certain point in his career the tide turned and from then on, everything seemed to work against him, until finally he had to accept the inevitable that he was a doomed man.

Ahab had supreme confidence in his prophets. Jehoshaphat, who began to be a little leery of them, finally realized that these prophets were not prophets of the Lord. Somewhat disturbed, he inquired, "*Is there* not still a prophet of the LORD here, that we may inquire of Him?" (I Ki. 22:7). Ahab frowned when he heard this, for he knew such a man, Micaiah, but he hated him because he prophesied only bad things. Jehoshaphat insisted, and Micaiah was brought out. The messenger sent to procure Micaiah told him, "Now listen, the words of the prophets with one accord encourage the king. Please, let your word be like the word of one of them, and speak encouragement" (I Ki. 22:13).

But Micaiah was not a prophet who could be bought. He, too, had a word; and his word was from the Lord. He saw the men of Israel scattered on the hills and their master missing. He was not afraid to tell the king the truth, although he knew that to do so was at the risk of his own life. He then related to Ahab and Jehoshaphat the strange scene he had seen in the spirit realm.

We see that even the evil spirits may go no further than they are permitted. For the sake of Jehoshaphat, God was making known the truth. If Ahab had had enough sense to accept Micaiah's warning, his life would have been saved. But he preferred to give heed to his hired prophets. The lying spirits had put lies in the mouth of Ahab's prophets. They had evidently secured Ahab's confidence, but now was the time to practice their deception and lead Ahab to his doom.

Ahab sentenced Micaiah to a bread-and-water diet in prison, and in a fool's euphoria, continued his plans, confident of victory. But his plans led to his death in battle. His execrable wife, Jezebel, suffered an ignominious death soon after.

It is important to note that lying spirits have God-given boundaries. Christ said, "If *it were* possible, they shall deceive the very elect" (Matt. 24:24 KJV). God is guarding the interests of His elect, even as He did for His servant Jehoshaphat. In the days preceding the great battle of Armageddon, these lying spirits will be permitted to go forth and gather the armies of the nations "to the battle of that great day of God Almighty" (Rev. 16:14).

And I saw three unclean spirits like frogs *coming* out of

the mouth of the dragon, out of the mouth of the beast, and out of the mouth of the false prophet. For they are spirits of demons, performing signs, *which* go out to the kings of the earth and of the whole world, to gather them to the battle of that great day of God Almighty (Rev. 16:13,14).

The number of lying spirits which are abroad these days deceiving people and leading them into darkness indicates that the great showdown of Armageddon is not far off.

Seducing Spirits

Now the Spirit expressly says that in latter times some will depart from the faith, giving heed to deceiving spirits and doctrines of demons, speaking lies in hypocrisy, having their own conscience seared with a hot iron (I Tim. 4:1,2).

Seducing spirits are a special kind of deceptive demon; their function is to lead people away from the truth into false doctrine. Paul mentions a few examples, such as "forbidding to marry, *and ...* to abstain from meats" (I Tim. 4:3). As we know, there are denominations which forbid their ministers to marry, which often leads to immorality and various deviations. There are other groups which teach that it is a sin to eat meat and contend that people should be restricted to a vegetarian diet.

But these are sidelines; the real object of seducing spirits is to influence people to depart from the faith. Paul remarks that in the last days men will have a "form of godliness but denying its power" (II Tim. 3:5). These people are characterized as "haughty, lovers of pleasure rather than lovers of God" (II Tim. 3:4). All such are influenced by the doctrines of seducing spirits. Ostensibly these "ministers of light" are not opposers of religion, but rather they substitute a false form of it which the Bible characterizes as apostate.

Peter warns of these false teachers and false prophets.

But there were also false prophets among the people,

even as there will be false teachers among you, who will secretly bring in destructive heresies, even denying the Lord who bought them, *and* bring on themselves swift destruction. And many will follow their destructive ways, because of whom the way of truth will be blasphemed (II Pet. 2:1,2).

Peter condemns such teachers in rather harsh words, comparing them to Balaam, the hireling prophet, and saying, "These are wells without water, clouds carried by a tempest, for whom is reserved the blackness of darkness forever (II Pet. 2:17).

Jude also warns against these men and exhorts the saints to contend earnestly for the faith, adding:

For certain men have crept in unnoticed, who long ago were marked out for this condemnation, ungodly men, who turn the grace of our God into lewdness and deny the only Lord God and our Lord Jesus Christ (Jude 4).

Jude compares them to Balaam who went greedily after reward. He misused his gift and turned to enchantments. In the end, Balaam became a common soothsayer and was slain by the children of Israel (Josh. 13:22). A soothsayer is one who practices divination with familiar spirits.

False religions and cults spring up as a result of people being deceived by seducing spirits. One minister we know was considered sound in his teachings many years ago. He now is the victim of seducing spirits. His most recent "revelations" are so ludicrous that it seems foolish even to take notice of them. He contends that scientists, geologists, explorers and air pilots are all in gigantic conspiracy to conceal the truth about the North and South Poles, where there is a hole that descends to the center of the earth — the location of both paradise and the bottomless pit. And the interior sun, he claims, illuminates this region where the wicked and even Satan will be converted in a few centuries. The man is the victim of seducing spirits, which have led him into the depths of delusion.

Seducing spirits on occasion may work very subtly, and are busy today seeking to influence and sidetrack men and women who are being used of God. They will endeavor to lead the person out of the mainstream of Christianity into some sideline that substantially or altogether cancels his effectiveness or causes him to repudiate his whole faith and take up with some occult religion.

The Demon of Murder

Among the demons that took possession of King Saul was a murderous demon. It is one thing to be envious or jealous of another person; it is another thing to want to kill him. But the relation between the two is nearer than is generally realized. When these passions dominate the human heart, the door is open to the murder demon. This is clearly exemplified in the life of Saul. When "the Spirit of the LORD departed from Saul, and a distressing spirit from the LORD troubled him" (I Sam. 16:14). At that time, the demon did not yet have a strong grip on the king, and when David played on his harp the songs of Zion, the spirit of worship drove away the oppressing spirit (vs. 23).

Later however, when David became popular in Israel after slaying Goliath, the king became exceedingly jealous. A murderous spirit entered into him, and he attempted to kill David with his javelin (I Sam. 18:11,12). Later, Saul made an attempt to murder his own son Jonathan (I Sam. 20:30-33).

The firstborn of the human race was a murderer; he slew his brother Abel in a fit of jealousy and rage. The inference is that a murderous demon took possession of Cain, "*who* was of the wicked one" because of his hatred for his brother:

> In this the children of God and the children of the devil are manifest: Whoever does not practice righteousness is not of God, nor is he who does not love his brother. For this is the message that you heard from the beginning, that we should love one another, not as Cain *who* was of the wicked one and murdered his brother. And why did he murder him? Because his works were evil

and his brother's righteous (I Jn. 3:10-12).

The average person finds it hard to conceive of circumstances which would drive him to take a human life. And yet most murders are not committed by professional criminals, but by relatives or acquaintances of the victim.

Abimelech, the son of Gideon's concubine, had ruthless ambition that caused him to murder 70 of his brothers. It is implied that his treacherous act was caused by a murderous spirit which not only dominated him, but in the end came between him and his own men of Shechem (Judg. 9:23).

John the apostle said, "Whoever hates his brother is a murderer" (I Jn. 3:15). When these passions of hatred are allowed full sway, they permit demon powers to gain entrance into the heart. Thus begins a vicious cycle, for demons increase their hold until they have the victim completely under their power.

The William Heirens case involved a series of heinous crimes that rocked Chicago many years ago. After his capture, young Heirens was given a "truth serum." While under the influence of the drug, a remarkable confession came forth which revealed a Dr. Jekyll and Mr. Hyde case all over again. Heirens blamed the crimes on another person whom he called "George Murman," and who he claimed lived inside him.

This evil personality apparently took possession of young Heirens after he had seen the film *Dr. Jekyll and Mr. Hyde*. In interviews with Lucy Freeman, a noted woman psychiatrist, he discussed his dual personality, and in a very confused state of mind, said of George: "I cannot put my finger where he is at, or where he is, but to me he seems just as real as if he is here." While under the influence of the "truth serum," he told how he tried to "make George a good boy," but that George always insisted on having his own way.

So real was this person to Heirens that when he was captured, they found a letter addressed to George Murman on his person. Heirens described George as "having red eyes, being about six feet tall, combs his hair straight back, and slicks it down with oil."

When asked if this man was a part of him, his answer was, "He has to be a part of me." Lucy Freeman, who had many interviews with Heirens and made a detailed study of the strange case, expressed certainty that the boy was schizophrenic, a split personality. During the interviews, Heirens, far from being a wild man, seemed to be an earnest youth sincerely interested in learning why he did certain things. At times, he was convinced that he had nothing to do with the murders; it was George Murman who was responsible. Yet at other times, he admitted that he must have been the one who committed the crimes.

Mrs. Freeman, in diagnosing the strange case, called special attention to the writing on the wall in lipstick that was left by the murderer after he had killed one of his victims. The scrawled note shows a split personality — man and demon. It read:

> For heaven's sake catch me before I kill more. I can't control myself.

Psychiatrists in most cases do not admit the existence of demons. Therefore, Mrs. Freeman lacked a vital link in her attempt to analyze the condition of young Heirens.

It would seem that even if we did not have the Bible to go by, the evidence would be irresistible that there are malicious spirits who get control of human beings and cause them to do terrible things. In Heirens' case, it was a murder demon.

Chapter Eleven

Stages of Demonic Control: Oppression, Obsession and Possession

We have now come to the subject of demon activity in its various forms, which includes progressively oppression, depression, obsession and possession. It is a matter of grave concern to understand the number of ways that demons are attacking, harassing and actually dominating people who are professing Christians. Unfortunately, there is a vast amount of ignorance regarding this vital subject. Many are confused on the manner of Satan's operations in this respect.

First of all, it is certainly not the will of God for the believer to be under Satan's oppression in any way — no, not for a moment! Satan is a defeated foe as far as the believer is concerned, and he should have no part in a life that is under the protection of the blood of Jesus. However, the devil respects nothing but force, and he will intrude anywhere and take advantage of anyone who will not stand up for his rights as a believer. The devil even attacked Christ, but was unable to touch Him because He refused to accept Satan's suggestions, resisting Him through the sword of the Spirit, which is the Word of God. Then Jesus could say, "The ruler of this world is coming, and he has nothing in Me" (Jn. 14:30). The devil should have "nothing" in the believer either.

> We know that whoever is born of God does not sin; but he who has been born of God keeps himself, and the wicked one does not touch him. We know that we are of God, and the whole world lies *under the sway of* the wicked one (I Jn. 5:18,19).

Sin is the main avenue through which the devil can attack people. The believer therefore must keep himself from evil, so the wicked one will not be able to touch him. The latter part of this passage says "the whole world lies *under the sway of* the wicked one." It is because of the prevalence of evil in this world that the devil is able to make such inroads against the human race.

The subject of demonic oppression is one that is greatly misunderstood by Christians. People confuse the terms — demon oppression, demon obsession and demon possession. In so doing, they are often led into error and false conclusions concerning this subject.

We must begin by declaring it is not the will of God for a believer to be under Satan's oppression in any form or way. This refers principally to demonic oppression, since Satan exercises his power and extends his sway largely through his vast army of evil spirits. Satan is a defeated foe, as far as the Christian is concerned. The devil sought to tempt Christ on various occasions, but never once did he succeed in getting Him to yield. Satan was unable to touch Him because He was wholly committed to the will of the Father and refused to hearken to his solicitations. The Lord resisted the enemy through the sword of the Spirit saying, "It is written." So as the shadow of the cross loomed before Him, Jesus could say, "The ruler of this world is coming, and he has nothing in Me" (Jn. 14:30).

How does Satan get control of a human being? Certainly he cannot go up to a person and just take over. He would like to do this if he could, but the human body is so created by God as to possess certain barriers that resist the intrusion of alien spirits. Ordinarily a period of time is required for Satan to get full control of a person, and he begins generally with the mind. He whispers a subtle suggestion, and if it is accepted, he gets a little foothold. He then goes on from there.

Sinners are naturally vulnerable to Satan's attacks, but the person may, if he chooses, reject his suggestions. Man has a conscience and the power of a will. He has power to reject Satan and choose right. If a person rejects Christ, the demonic influences gradually increase their pressure, and if no change of attitude occurs, chains are forged that eventually cannot be broken by human power. The importance of being born again and accepting Christ into every department of one's life is clear from I John 5:18,19.

Certainly the person has something to do. "We know that whoever is born of God does not sin; but he who has been born of God keeps himself, and the wicked one does not touch him" (I Jn. 5:18). We are told to resist the devil and he will flee from us (Jas. 4:7). I John 5:19 is of solemn import: "We know that we are of God, and the whole world lies *under the sway of* the wicked one."

It is because of the prevalence of evil in the world that Satan is able to create such havoc within the human race. The only antidote is repentance and the new birth. We cannot exorcise the devil from a sinner; there must be a change of heart. If the enemy is cast out and the heart is unchanged, it would only be an invitation for the devil to return. Thus to secure deliverance from the oppression of Satan, we seek first to bring men to repentance.

> In humility correcting those who are in opposition, if God perhaps will grant them repentance, so that they may know the truth, and *that* they may come to their senses *and escape* the snare of the devil, having been taken captive by him to *do* his will (II Tim. 2:25,26).

True repentance is one of the greatest means of exorcising Satan's grip upon a life.

Demonic Oppression

Satan's initial method of approach is usually through the mind. He cannot take possession of either the mind or body by direct action. His domination of the lives of myriads of people happens through a process that requires time. If the individual deliberately refuses to accept Christ into his life, the demon will gradually exercise a stronger control, until the bondage is such that it cannot be broken by human power.

There is such a thing as absolute demon possession, as was the case of the man living among the tombs (Mk. 5:1-20). That man was completely insane. It is not Satan's aim to take such absolute control over all people. A lunatic is unable to promote the devil's cause beyond providing a habitation for one or more of his evil spirits. The devil seeks to influence people's minds to the point that they disbelieve God's Word and live a worldly life. If he succeeds in this, he knows that eventually they will go to a Christless grave — his real objective. To liberate people from present and future demonic influence, it is important to bring them to repentance before God.

Under Satan's sinister influence, the soul without God steadily gravitates into sin and gradually loses all taste for spiritual things. In this condition, he will never seek after God unless the Word of God comes to him, quickened by the Holy Spirit.

> And you *He made alive*, who were dead in trespasses and sins, in which you once walked according to the course of this world, according to the prince of the power of the air, the spirit who now works in the sons of disobedience (Eph. 2:1,2).

The awakened sinner then realizes that he must make a decision. The decision he makes will influence his life not only for time, but for eternity. In this life, it will determine whether he will be a free man or a slave to demon power.

Demonic Oppression of the Mind

When the human mind is not in harmony with the revealed will of God, it is particularly open to suggestions from evil spirits. Making suggestions is the first step in the enemy's strategy to control the mind. How quickly Satan was able to influence Peter. He had just made the great confession of Christ's deity, which had been revealed to him by God (Matt. 16:16,17). Yet a short while later under the influence of the devil, Peter took it upon himself to rebuke the Lord and advise Him that He was not to die upon the cross (Matt. 16:22). Isaiah 53 tells of the sufferings of the Messiah Who was to come, but Peter did not see it that way. He wanted the Lord to set up His throne on earth immediately. This suggestion did not come from God; it came from Satan.

Notice the significance of Christ's answer. His reply was not to Peter, but to Satan!

> He turned and said to Peter, "Get behind Me, Satan! You are an offense to Me, for you are not mindful of the things of God, but the things of men" (Matt. 16:23).

Because Peter was so carnal, the devil was able to make his suggestion to Peter without his being aware of who gave it to him. Small wonder then that Christians today who live on a carnal plane receive and accept many suggestions from the devil.

Jesus always tested the suggestions that came to Him by measuring them with the Word of God. Consequently, the devil was unable to get anywhere with Him. "For as he (a man) thinks in his heart, so *is* he" (Prov. 23:7), said the inspired writer.

The secret of continuous victory is to guard the gates of the mind so that the enemy cannot intrude. But many Christians fail at this point. The devil tells the young convert that he has lost "the feeling" and therefore is no longer saved. He suggests to the one who has been healed that the symptoms of his disease are coming back. In either case, if his suggestions are listened to and accepted, the enemy follows up on his advantage at once. The devil's plan is to get people to live in the negative, for in so doing they become a target for his suggestions. Even though the believer may still hold to his faith in Christ, if he gives heed to these suggestions, he will lose the victory and help to swell the ranks of the army of neurotic Christians.

What is the answer? Victory lies in the spirit and in the mind. Our warfare is not against flesh and blood, but against unseen spiritual powers. We must reject their suggestions, casting them down as imaginations that spring from our enemy, Satan.

> Casting down arguments and every high thing that exalts itself against the knowledge of God, bringing every thought into captivity to the obedience of Christ (II Cor. 10:5).

The answer to negative thinking is not to have a blank mind; it is to think positive thoughts. If we think God's thoughts, negative thoughts will have no place. In the book of Philippians, the Apostle Paul tells us what God's thoughts are:

> Finally, brethren, whatever things are true, whatever things *are* noble, whatever things *are* just, whatever things *are* pure, whatever things *are* lovely, whatever things *are* of good report, if *there is* any virtue and if *there is* anything praiseworthy — meditate on these things (Phil. 4:8).

Demonic Obsession

Demon oppression is Satan's first step in seeking control of a human being. It varies in intensity and effectiveness in different persons, but if the individual makes no serious attempt to resist the evil powers, inevitably Satan's grip becomes stronger and stronger. This is a more dangerous condition than oppression. When a person is oppressed of the enemy, he still has control of his faculties and can choose to be delivered from his condition. In demon obsession, the person comes under the spell of his delusion and does not wish to be freed from it. In fact, he is now its willing victim and desires the perpetuation of the evil thing that has come into his life. Demon obsession is not quite the same as demon possession, but it is an escape from reality and can, and often does, lead to this final state.

When a person is "neurotic," evidence is that Satan has increased his hold to the point that his thinking in some channels has become seriously distorted. The number of neurotics in this country is far greater than is generally supposed. Some put the number as high as one in 10. A neurotic is sane in most respects, but on some line tends to act irrationally with abnormal conduct. Satan in such cases has usually succeeded in securing a hold strong enough on the person that he is no longer a happy, normal individual. Unfortunately among this company are not a few professing Christians, some of whom are verging on a mental breakdown.

Obsession is far more serious than is oppression. The person may still be recognized as legally sane, but his thinking on certain lines is dangerously warped and distorted. He is well on his way to a paranoic condition which will bring his sanity into serious question.

A person who is oppressed by an evil spirit may recognize his condition and fervently desire deliverance. Unfortunately, when a person reaches a state of obsession, he is for all practical purposes mentally unsound. He often does not wish deliverance because he fervently believes in or wishes to harbor his delusions.

The classic illustration in the Scriptures of obsession is the case of King Saul. Even though the demon of jealousy which troubled him had been exorcised several times through David's anointed playing of the harp, Saul continued to brood over his misfortunes. True to the symptoms of his disease, he imagined that his troubles were caused by David rather than himself. As a consequence of his constant brooding, he invited the demon to return. As the demon increased his hold upon Saul, he became obsessed with the desire to kill David, the one who had done him a great service by slaying the giant Goliath, and who had challenged the armies of Israel.

Saul never did rid himself of this obsession, but continued on in his mad course, pursuing David and abandoning himself to his elemental emotions, until finally the Spirit of the Lord departed from him altogether. His act on the final night of his life was to consult a witch in an attempt to communicate with Samuel, long dead.

Spiritualists and their devotees are victims of delusions caused by seducing spirits. Although the Bible condemns attempted communication with the dead and attaches the severest of penalties, spiritualists find a way of rationalizing all this. They persuade themselves that these spirits are what they claim to be, despite the fact that familiar spirits are notorious liars. Only the power of God can deliver those who become obsessed with this powerful delusion.

There are many other deceptions perhaps less dangerous than spiritualism victimizing people today. Some Christians become obsessed with teachings patently at variance with the Scriptures, holding to them with great tenacity. Some of these doctrines might be harmless were it not that they divide the Church. Others are definitely of the spirit of anti-Christ and lead their devotees to spiritual ruin.

I recall an instance of a woman who was trying to persuade us to accept a certain "revelation" which she claimed to have received. I pointed out that the Scriptures did not back up her "revelation." She told me that this "new light" was received only by special dispensation. I replied perhaps a little sternly (though I did not mean to be harsh, but I felt under the circumstances that it was necessary to be very plain) that she had indeed seen a light, but not the light of the Word of God, rather "the glow from the bottomless pit." She was, of course, not happy over this remark.

In almost all cases, those who come under the spell of any of these doctrinal obsessions consider their doctrine more important than anything else, and in fact, regard belief in them as the acid test of fellowship. The thing has become a fixation in their mind, and usually they are not content unless they are proselytizing others to their peculiar obsession.

Demonic Possession of the Body

We now come to the matter of actual demon possession — the most deadly form of demon activity, and a subject of which there is considerable misunderstanding. To properly understand the manner in which Satan operates in this field, we must recognize what is clearly taught in the Scriptures — that man is a threefold being. Therefore, any of these facets of his nature are in danger of being attacked by the enemy. Fortunately, God has provided ample means by which the believer can be made completely secure against all attacks by the enemy.

> Behold, I give you the authority to trample on serpents and scorpions, and over all the power of the enemy, and nothing shall by any means hurt you (Lk. 10:19).

Attacks of demons begin against the physical body, and from there proceed to the more dangerous phases of demon possession. Earlier, we noted that evil spirits can oppress or actually possess one or more organs of the human body by settling on the vital nerves of those organs. It is clearly possible for believers to become a victim of the physical oppression of demons — but only if those believers, through ignorance or wrong teaching, fail to take their rightful authority over the devil. It is taught by the Scriptures that it is not God's will that Satan should have any power over the believers (I Jn. 5:18,19). Nevertheless, while Christians are regularly taught that one should put his soul in the hands of God, unfortunately not all are taught that we must also put our bodies in the hands of God.

That the devil can take possession of the body without affecting the soul and spirit is clearly shown in I Corinthians 5. The believer Paul speaks of here had fallen into sin of the darkest hue, for he was having sexual relations with his own father's wife. Paul delivered this man over to Satan for the "destruction" of his body so that as a result of the ordeal his spirit would be saved.

> In the name of our Lord Jesus Christ, when you are gathered together, along with my spirit, with the power of our Lord Jesus Christ, deliver such a one to Satan for the destruction of the flesh, that his spirit may be saved in the day of the Lord Jesus (I Cor. 5:4,5).

It is probable that some professing Christians are suffering bodily affliction for a similar cause. They have disobeyed God or are tolerating known sin in their life. Certainly, however, the above instance is no reason for a sincere believer to be under the oppression of the devil. In this case, the affliction came upon the man because of his deeds. Paul gave him a taste of the devil's power so that he would repent, turn from evil and be saved.

To defeat an enemy we must first be able to recognize and

identify his activities. That evil spirits are the cause of many afflictions is plainly taught by the Scriptures. Christ cast evil spirits out of the deaf, the blind and the infirm. Yet Christians who have these afflictions are sometimes offended by the implication that their sickness could be caused by evil spirits, since they are convinced that no evil spirit can touch a Christian.

But what do the Scriptures say? Jesus cast an infirm spirit out of the body of a woman whom He spoke of as a believer, "a daughter of Abraham" (Lk. 13:16). When Jesus referred to people as being sons or daughters of Abraham, He meant their spiritual relationship (Jn. 8:39) not natural descent (Jn. 8:37). This woman was a daughter of Abraham by the flesh and also by faith. Nevertheless, an infirm spirit had taken residence in the nervous system of her back, causing her to be bowed over in a most distressing position. Jesus cast the devil out — much to the annoyance of the ruler of the synagogue, an ecclesiastic who apparently was not interested in his parishioners being freed from evil spirits, at least not on the Sabbath day. Jesus told him that he was more interested in seeing his ox watered on the Sabbath day than this woman being delivered from the bonds of Satan (Lk. 13:15,16).

Just as this daughter of Abraham suffered physically from the tyranny of Satan, so today there are many of Abraham's sons and daughters by faith (Rom. 4:16) who are oppressed in body by the enemy. They have not learned that the devil has no right to do so, and they have not stood on their rights.

Demonic Possession of the Brain

That there is a difference between the human mind and the brain is shown in the symptoms of the disease of epilepsy. Epilepsy is a name for various disorders in which the electrical rhythms of the central nervous system are disturbed, causing convulsions and clouded consciousness. According to the Scriptures, demons can cause epileptic seizures (Lk. 9:39). As with blindness, deafness, etc., epilepsy can also come about due to causes other than demonic activity.

The boy in Luke 9 who fell into the water and the fire was a victim of an epileptic demon. When a demon spirit possesses a willing victim such as a spiritualist medium, it enters into a kind of covenant relationship with the person. In the case of an epileptic who is being attacked by a demon, however, the demon seizes the mind against the will of the person, who sincerely desires deliverance. Some Christians do have epileptic seizures. If it is caused by an evil spirit tormenting them, it will be unable to possess their souls, though it injures their bodies.

In spiritualism, the medium enters into a sort of covenant relationship with the familiar spirit, which acts as a "control" in the impersonations carried on during trances. In return for the privilege of habitation, this evil spirit allows the medium to retain possession of his faculties, except when he is in a trance. His alleged communication with the dead is one of the devil's schemes to draw people away from the Word of God and under the influence of seducing spirits.

Absolute Demonic Possession — Insanity

Absolute demon possession generally means insanity. Usually the symptoms develop in slow stages and increase in character, especially if more than one evil spirit takes possession of the individual. The uncontrolled emotions of suspicion, jealousy, envy, bitterness and hatred open the door to these unclean spirits. Instead of recognizing their danger and seeking help from God, people who come under the influence of this kind of oppression are inclined to brood over their troubles and thus encourage the very thing that seeks their ruin. Due to the negative attitude they assume, the way may be opened for more than one evil spirit to enter. This process may develop to the point where the person becomes violently insane. Since such victims resist any assistance and actually wish to live in their world of delusion, there is little that can be done for them. Notwithstanding, it is a matter of record that the power of God has delivered many such cases.

Psychiatry is the modern profession which seeks to assist people with sick minds or those who are maladjusted. Psychiatrists have no power to cast out evil spirits, but must work as a physician on the natural plane. They seek to help the person to recognize the basic cause of their frustrations. Hours of consultation over a period of many months are often required in the effort to trace the unpleasant circumstance in a person's youth that is responsible for the frustration. Sometimes psychiatrists are able to uncover a cause long buried in the mind, and in so doing, they release the pent up neurosis. The person may then show improvement.

Man was made in the image of God. It was the divine purpose that man become a habitation of God, a temple of the Spirit of God. "Do you not know that your body is the temple of the Holy Spirit *who is* in you, whom you have from God, and you are not your own?" (I Cor. 6:19). If an individual closes his nature to God and opens it to evil, those powers will enter and, in time, take possession of the person's faculties. Judas Iscariot was perhaps one of the most notorious examples.

There are many differences in degree and kind of demonic activity. Some persons are completely possessed, yet harmless to others. In many instances, however, a person becomes violent and proves a menace to society, requiring confinement in a mental institution. In any case, it is a sad and tragic thing to see a person made in the image of God robbed of his dominion and, like Samson of old, made a slave to evil powers who are interested only in his ruin.

Exhibitionism — Sign of Demon Possession

The demon-possessed man spoken of in Mark 5 clothed himself immediately after deliverance. Public nudity is almost a certain sign of demon possession, and is becoming common these days.

One of the most startling cases of exhibitionism that ever came to our attention was that of a man who visited a church we pastored years ago. On the surface, the man seemed to be normal. In fact, he held a position of trust in a large religious organization. Under the respectable facade he presented, there lurked a raging demon. We could scarcely believe our ears when we heard that in the next city he had been caught and arrested in the act of exhibiting himself to some young girls. How powerful must have been the sinister drive for him to commit an act that in one moment tore down everything he had built up in a lifetime, bringing shame upon his wife and family.

In recent years, there has been a steady moral deterioration of society. Masses of people seem to be under the influence of exhibitionist demons. At outdoor rock festivals, it is not unusual for a number of young people to disrobe completely. Nudity is now common on some beaches. Thousands of young women shamelessly expose their bodies to supply pornographic photos. Due to the decision of the U.S. Supreme Court, pornographic films and plays in which the vilest perversions are performed are allowed in "adult theaters."

As in the case of the demons Jesus cast out of the lunatic, which swarmed over the swine causing them to panic and stampede to their destruction, demons today seem to swarm en masse over humanity that has sold itself to sensuality, driving it to madness and to the most extreme acts of depravity. Only human beings in the lowest stages of moral degeneration seek to expose themselves.

The Final Fate of the Demons

What is the future of the demonic hosts? What will be their fate? One of the most fearsome events involving demons will occur during the great and terrible day of the Lord. It will be the incursion of demons from the bottomless pit. Apparently there is a great number of these spirits presently incarcerated in the pit (also called the abyss), a place of imprisonment of spirits. Just why some demons are free and others are imprisoned is not clear; but at the sounding of the fifth trumpet, the bottomless pit will be opened, and these malicious spirits will be permitted to escape to conduct new mischief upon earth (Rev. 9:1-11). When we consider the extent of evil that the demon spirits now roaming the earth are able to inflict upon humanity, we can only imagine the fearful result of these vast reinforcements of the hosts of hell being released.

The appearance of these demons from the pit is like that of locusts. But they are not ordinary locusts, for the description given of their activities is something entirely different. Ordinary locusts attack the green vegetation, but these do not hurt "the grass of the earth, or any green thing" (Rev. 9:4). They have a grievous power to afflict the wicked, tormenting them but not producing death. Their activities are controlled by Abaddon, the angel of the bottomless pit. Since the great and terrible day of the Lord does not occur until following the Great Tribulation and the final harvest of God's elect, the saints will not be affected by this terrible judgment; but woe to those who reject the Gospel and remain on earth during these terrible days.

The demons know that they have a limited period of freedom on earth. When Jesus met the lunatic in which a legion of demons dwelt, the demons cried out, "Have You come here to torment us before the time?" (Matt. 8:29). Adam and Eve (mankind) had received authority over the earth, but their sin allowed for that authority to be transferred to Satan; from that time, the kingdom of darkness has been exercising dominion over the earth. But their time is at last drawing to a close. After the judgments of the day of the Lord, Satan and his followers will be cast into the bottomless pit.

> Then I saw an angel coming down from heaven, having the key to the bottomless pit and a great chain in his hand. He laid hold of the dragon, that serpent of old, who is *the* Devil and Satan, and bound him for a thousand years; and he cast him into the bottomless pit, and shut him up, and set a seal on him, so that he should deceive the nations no more till the thousand years were finished. But after these things he must be released for a little while (Rev. 20:1-3).

After the thousand years are finished, Satan will be loosed for a little season to test the inhabitants of the earth born during the millennium. Following that he will be cast into the lake of fire.

The devil, who deceived them, was cast into the lake of fire and brimstone where the beast and the false prophet *are*. And they will be tormented day and night forever and ever (Rev. 20:10).

That this same judgment will be inflicted upon the followers of Satan is explicitly stated in Matthew 25:41:

Then He will also say to those on the left hand, "Depart from Me, you cursed, into the everlasting fire prepared for the devil and his angels."

Thus will end the regime of this wicked archangel, but as Jesus said, "the righteous (go) into eternal life" (Matt. 25:46).

Part III:

Demonic Manifestations and Delusions

Chapter Twelve

Spirit Phenomena as Revealed in the Scriptures

The Scriptures teach that under certain circumstances, Satan and his host of evil spirits are able to produce visible spirit phenomena which cannot be accounted for by natural means. Most of these manifestations require the demonic possession or control of a human body. Without embodiment, evil spirits are greatly, if not altogether, restricted in their activities upon the earth. Satan was able to deceive Eve by embodying himself in a serpent. (This beast was at that time quite different in form than after it was cursed.)

Satan's preternatural manifestations have one purpose: to deceive people into believing the manifestations are of God, and thereby lead them into error. Had Eve known that it was Satan who was conversing with her, she would have fled for her life. But she was beguiled by him and led astray.

The Magic of Egypt

Pharaoh's sorcerers were able to duplicate Aaron's feat when he cast his rod upon the ground, and it became a serpent. However, Aaron's rod swallowed the rods of the magicians (Ex. 7:12), indicating that while Satan can imitate certain aspects of God's power, the Almighty's power is always supreme.

Pharaoh's enchanters were also able to turn the waters of the Nile

River into blood like Aaron did (Ex. 7:22). Apparently, Satan desired to make it appear that Moses had the same kind of magic Pharaoh's witch doctors and magicians had. Next, the Egyptian magicians produced frogs, copying Aaron and Moses (Ex. 8:7). But there was a limit to the magicians' power. When they tried to duplicate Aaron's feat of bringing forth lice, they failed (Ex. 8:18).

At this point, the enchanters apparently became convinced that Aaron and Moses' power was of God (Ex. 8:19). Pharaoh was too stubborn to concede this, thus inviting further judgments upon his land. The magicians had played out their enchantments, for when the plague of boils came, they were stricken and could get no relief (Ex. 9:11). In some cases, the magicians had power to invoke a curse, but they had no power to remove it.

Witchcraft — Spiritualistic Mediums

Witchcraft was practiced even in the earliest times. The law of Moses warned sternly against this practice: "You shall not permit a sorceress to live" (Ex. 22:18). During the time when King Saul was obedient, he carried out this law and banished witchcraft from the land. However, after Saul's long series of disobedient acts, the Lord forsook him and "did not answer him" (I Sam. 28:6). The king decided to consult the witch of En Dor, a woman possessed with a familiar spirit (I Sam. 28:7) in an attempt to communicate with Samuel in the realm of the dead.

A familiar spirit is supposedly the spirit of a dead person invoked by a medium to advise or prophesy to the living. In most cases, this communication is nothing but a base deception. Evil spirits know the habits of individuals during their lifetime, and they are able to copy the tone of the person's voice through the medium. The listeners are deluded into believing that they are actually listening to the dead person represented. Those deceived in this manner are responsible for being misled because they have disobeyed the Scriptures, which expressly forbid attempting to communicate with the dead. Judgment came upon Saul's house for his sins, one of which was his attempt to communicate with Samuel through a witch:

So Saul died for his unfaithfulness which he had committed against the LORD, because he did not keep the word of the LORD, and also because he consulted a medium for guidance (I Chr. 10:13).

There are many Bible scholars who believe that in this one case, God brought up from Sheol the real Samuel. If so, it is the only exception ever recorded.

There is an instance in the book of Acts of a girl "possessed with a spirit of divination ... who brought her masters much profit by fortune-telling" (Acts 16:16). The Apostle Paul, moved by the Spirit of God, rebuked the unclean spirit that possessed the girl, and she was no longer able to foretell events. The Bible plainly shows that these so-called psychic manifestations are in reality caused by evil spirits.

Satan demonstrated one of his more remarkable powers by taking Christ up onto a high mountain and showing Him "all the kingdoms of the world in a moment of time" (Lk. 4:5). Satan offered Jesus all the wealth and power on earth if He would worship him. Jesus answered him from the Word of God, indignantly rejecting his suggestion that He worship anyone other than the Lord God (Lk. 4:5-8).

The Apostle Paul expressly states that at the time of the Second Coming of Christ, Satan will empower "the lawless one" (John calls him the Antichrist) to produce "signs, and lying wonders."

> The coming of the *lawless one* is according to the working of Satan, with all power, signs, and lying wonders, and with all unrighteous deception among those who perish, because they did not receive the love of the truth, that they might be saved. And for this reason God will send them strong delusion, that they should believe the lie, that they all may be condemned who did not believe the truth but had pleasure in unrighteousness (II Thes. 2:9-12).

Supernatural satanic phenomena will greatly increase in the earth as the final Day of the Lord approaches. Jesus warned that the "signs and wonders" of false prophets and anti-Christs would be of such a nature that they would be able "to deceive, if possible, even the elect" (Matt. 24:24). The book of Revelation reveals that the false prophet will perform "great signs" (Rev. 13:13).

It will not be possible for the elect to be deceived, however, since they are forewarned by the Word of God. Those who are careless, however, will be fair game for the devil's delusions, and will be snared by him in great numbers. It is therefore important that we be aware of and able to recognize the devil's manifestations.

Chapter Thirteen

Case Studies of Delusions Caused by Seducing Spirits

The following are a number of cases in which I have observed seducing spirits. Many more instances might be cited, but these will be sufficient to suit our purpose.

Case I — The Deceiving Spirit

Shortly after my conversion, I began setting aside certain periods of time to seek the Lord. My heart was hungry for a deeper revelation of God's wisdom and power. During this period, another brother often spent considerable time with me in prayer. Bill seemed quite sincere. Some time later, I learned that Bill periodically indulged in drinking strong liquor, at which time he became quite another man. Actually, I believe that Bill desired to be a real Christian. But when temptation pressed him, he would yield to it, thus opening the door to demonic powers.

One night while we were praying, Bill began to hear a voice. The voice claimed to be of God, and it informed him that he had been specially favored of God to receive certain "revelations." Bill was far from an educated person, and the "revelations" he received indicated that another intelligence was doing the speaking. In fact, most of the subjects discussed were well beyond his knowledge. Subjects such as heaven and hell were minutely discussed and described in detail. Being a new Christian, I was fascinated by all this, and I had no doubt the communications were of God. Having reached the place where we had unreserved confidence in the "messages," the voice then began to play on our egos. Foolishly, we were elated over the thought of being the recipients of revelations that seemed to be as great as those in the Bible.

Then came the ultimate "revelation." Bill was told that he was "Elijah" returned to earth! (Poor Elijah! How many people in the course of history have supposed that they were Elijah, and have gone to extreme efforts to prove the alleged identity!) Bill was convinced that he was Elijah, and the voice warned me that I must accept him as God's special prophet. Naive as I was, for the first time I began to entertain suspicions. When this young man began to publicly declare his office as the prophet, I finally realized that something was definitely wrong. I did not yet know about Bill's addiction to alcohol and his periodic relapses — which made the operation of seducing spirits possible.

When I became convinced that the voice must either be a seducing or a familiar spirit, I was shocked to realize that I had been so easily deceived. I then earnestly pleaded with him to seek God for deliverance from the deceiving spirit. He was willing to listen, and we knelt together to pray. But the voice warned us with great urgency that all was well — as long as we did not doubt. It proclaimed, "I will prove to you that I am of God." At that very moment, a guitar standing in the corner made a sound as if a hand had been drawn over its strings. This was repeated several times.

No longer deceived, I challenged the voice, declaring that it was not God but a familiar spirit. Unmasked, the devil said, "Yes, I am the devil. God has permitted me to deceive you because you have committed the unpardonable sin! You are forever lost!"

For several days, I was almost ready to believe this, and I went through great anguish of soul. However, God came to me with the following Scripture: "Let not your heart be troubled; you believe in

God, believe also in Me" (Jn. 14:1). The Lord then made me to know that He had permitted me to go through this experience so that I would not trust every spirit, but I would try the spirits and learn the difference between the true and the false. It was a valuable lesson for me in the years to come, and one that I have never forgotten.

Case II — The "Unpardonable Sin" Delusion

The fact that these demons afflict some good Christians is a plain fact. We must not, as the ostrich does, put our heads in the sand and ignore the facts; instead we must take measures and instruct others that they do not fall victim to Satan's wiles. The victim in this instance was a person close to our family — so close we called her "grandmother." The devil deluded her by telling her she had committed the unpardonable sin, and she believed it.

Years previously, grandmother and her husband had lived in luxury. "Grandfather" operated a prosperous business. Apparently, however, he was not too shrewd of a businessman, and his assets gradually declined. They eventually had to move into a small house and get along in a very modest way. This was extremely mortifying to grandmother, who could never forget the days of their prosperity.

My parents gave them some help, but they had a large family and had about all they could do to take care of themselves. Worst of all, grandmother's pride was severely affected. She remembered the days when they held a prominent position in the community, and now they were struggling to survive. The most painful thing was that she had warned her husband against his improvident investments. He had not heeded her advice, and when these failed, the effect upon her was devastating.

Having been used to fine things, she constantly brooded over their misfortune. Instead of being thankful for the blessings she had received, she allowed herself to enter a state of chronic frustration. Somehow she felt that God had not been fair to her.

As the result of her constant worry, she broke down completely. She became irrational, and fell under the delusion that she had committed the unpardonable sin. Her constant brooding over financial reverses made conditions favorable for the enemy to obtain control of her mind.

I have no doubt concerning her salvation. In the past, she had placed her soul in the hands of God, and God does not forsake His children in adversity. Too bad she had not placed her mind in the hands of the Lord. She allowed fear to dominate her, and like Job, what she feared came upon her. She paid dearly because she did not take her refuge in the Lord as commanded in Philippians 4:6,7:

> Be anxious for nothing, but in everything by prayer and supplication, with thanksgiving, let your requests be made known to God; and the peace of God, which surpasses all understanding, will guard your hearts and minds through Christ Jesus.

If Christians would practice the truth of these words, there would be far fewer mental breakdowns among Christians. For when we violate these principles, Satan, ever alert, will not hesitate to make the most of his advantage.

Case III — Satanic Delusion of a False Religion

My wife relates a story which is one of the most bizarre of our entire experience. This sad event shows the extent and power of demonic delusion when the person deliberately ignores biblical warnings to test the spirits, and human pride blinds the individual to the nature of the deception.

"She was a beautiful girl — a rather tall, slender blonde. Her grace and charm won her many friends. Her musical talent gave her an open door of service. When she stood before an audience, she had a natural poise. Above and beyond all this, she was dedicated. She spent many of her Sunday afternoons at the church praying for the young people, whose meetings she led. Her entire family was spiritual and a credit to our church. She was an outstanding leader with a bright future.

"Our close contact with her was broken when we left that part of the country. We heard that she had gone to Los Angeles to attend

Bible school. But while in school, she made the mistake that many have made — she turned her eyes toward people instead of keeping them focused on Jesus. She became lonesome, disillusioned and discouraged — a fertile field for the devil to begin sowing his seeds of doubt and discontent.

"Next, she began attending a church whose standards were considerably lower than those upheld in her town. Then came the report that the pastor was keeping company with this blonde. How could this be? He was a married man with a family! But it was true. And finally, the news came that they had run away together!

"But the pastor's wife put the police on their trail, and shortly after, they were apprehended. The minister was put in jail and convicted of stealing. The car he had used to make his getaway was in his wife's name, and thus was her personal property.

"There in that jail was born one of the most satanically-inspired, false religions. The minister, instead of confessing and forsaking his sin, decided to go on a fast. The guilty would rather do most anything than to confess and forsake their sin. During his fast, a voice spoke to him and said, 'You must start a new religion. All other religions are wrong. The Christian faith is error. Christ is a bastard. You must overthrow them all. You must start this new doctrine now. Call this true religion Yahweh.'

"Immediately, he sent for his newly acquired wife. As he told her of his 'revelation,' a strange power came upon her — a strong delusion from hell — and she embraced this cult, utterly forsaking Christ! Since he had to serve out his term in the penitentiary, who was to carry on in the meantime? She was, of course!

"And so it was, after our party had just completed a large salvation-healing revival in Los Angeles, we picked up the local paper and there beheld an announcement of a Sunday afternoon service by this strange cult. I felt I must attend and see for myself, as the reports were hard to believe about one who had been so close to us.

"I slipped into a seat near the rear of the auditorium, breathing a prayer that I would go unnoticed. Several hundred people were present. Soon the service began. Someone led some songs, all of which were unfamiliar to me. At last, our friend made her way to the platform. There she stood, beautifully clothed in a long, shining garment, with a cluster of flowers on her left shoulder. All eyes were upon her!

"What I saw and heard during the next hour still brings cold chills to me, and will remain indelibly imprinted on my mind as long as I live! All at once, a spontaneous praise and worship of Yahweh broke forth from the people, as they rose to their feet with hands stretched toward heaven. This occurred again and again. I felt at times I must run from the building, the powers of darkness were so oppressive to me. But I decided to weather it, sitting silently with my hat somewhat pulled over my face to avoid recognition.

"And then came the sermon — a bitter attack against Christianity. The blond mistress stood there and cursed and blasphemed Christ, again and again, calling Him 'bastard,' while the congregation shouted, 'Praise Yahweh!' She read Scriptures from the Bible concerning the Holy Spirit, the Virgin Birth and the Resurrection. She would describe these events in a lewd manner, and pervert them into a sexual joke, amid a mighty roar of 'Praise Yahweh' from her adherents.

"At long last, the service came to a close. I stepped in line to shake hands with the speaker. When she recognized me, her face became ashen white, and she began to tremble. Calling me by my first name (which she had never before done), she asked, 'Were you in the service?' I told her I was. I then asked her to accompany us to dinner, as Brother Lindsay was to join me momentarily. She declined with many and varied excuses, but I insisted.

"Another hour passed, and it was apparent that our guest was stalling for time, hoping we would leave. She disappeared into a dressing room, outside of which we stationed ourselves, as the minutes ticked wearily away. Finally at long last, she emerged with several 'attendants,' who, she informed us, must accompany her. We drove to a restaurant, and there persuaded her to leave her 'escorts' in the car while we went in to eat.

"Then Brother Lindsay asked her if she had heard of our large meeting. No, she hadn't heard. Nor had she heard of other similar campaigns in various cities with many thousands attending. We assured her that the real Christian revival was just getting under way, thousands were getting saved and healed, and God was pouring out His Spirit. Her face registered surprise and bewilderment as we continued to show her the error of her decision. Then nervously, she quickly arose, shook hands with Brother Lindsay, threw her arms around me, hugged and kissed me, and walked away to join her 'escorts.'

"When we arrived back at our apartment, we prayed earnestly for her salvation and asked God to bring a halt to this terrible delusion which was spreading as a new religion. We stayed in the city another two weeks. Each Saturday, we would look for her ad. Each time, it stated, 'Due to the illness of (the young blonde) — no service will be held.' We learned later that week from a relative of hers, that immediately after she left us, she developed throat trouble and was unable to talk. We felt God had, at least temporarily, closed down her services while we were in the city.

"For a long time we had no further news concerning this cult, though occasionally we received a letter in our office from one who had fallen into the devil's trap.

> Because they did not receive the love of the truth, that they might be saved. And for this reason God will send them strong delusion, that they should believe the lie, that they all may be condemned who did not believe the truth but had pleasure in unrighteousness (II Thes. 2:10-12).

"Now comes the most startling development: I had been seeking information concerning the status of this movement, and also the sequel to what had happened to this young woman.

"I was dictating a letter to a Los Angeles newspaper for possible information, when our secretary, who had recently been a resident of Denver, suddenly paused and looked up in an excited manner, exclaiming, 'Why, I know what happened to that woman!' What she told me, shocked me beyond words! We wrote to the *Rocky Mountain News* in Denver, from which we learned that at the time this young woman disappeared from our contact, she had entered the entertainment field. In 1950, she was known in Houston as the 'Blonde Bombshell' in the various night clubs where she sang and played. After several years of nightlife, she decided to turn again to her strange religious delusion. However, by this time —

> She separated from her husband — and divorce proceedings were under way.
>
> Miss ___ leased her offices in Denver a week ago, with plans to lecture and write on psychic phenomena, stressing the use of extra-sensory perception. She planned to establish headquarters here for the Kingdom of Yahweh, a religious cult.
>
> She told police she was working late Friday, when she was accosted. ... She said the man raped her after smashing a pop bottle over her head, and striking her in the mouth and stomach. The assailant then knifed a janitor who came to her aid.
>
> One day later, on Sunday morning, Miss ___ was found by her hostess, with her feet resting on the bed, and her head and shoulders on the floor. It appeared she suffered a convulsion. Death occurred at 6:30 a.m. (Denver's *Rocky Mountain News*, March 4, 1957.)

"The *Rocky Mountain News* carried inch-tall headlines on the front page of Monday's paper — with a seven-inch photograph — saying, 'BLONDE MYSTIC DIES AFTER ASSAULT.' So ended the career of one who might have been greatly used of God, had she followed in His footsteps."

Case IV — The Deluded Evangelist

There was a man who possessed above-average ability, and his ministry, up to the time he gave heed to seducing spirits, showed considerable promise. However, he had a certain instability in his nature, and later it became apparent that he was moved by an ambition to ride higher and faster than his ministry warranted. Such individuals are often open to self-deceptions.

I had noted with some misgivings his occasional reports of alleged conversations with the "Angel Gabriel." Angelic visitation is clearly both an Old Testament and New Testament doctrine. However, angels usually appear to the humble, and their visitations are hardly for the purpose of providing promotional material for an overzealous evangelist. Nevertheless, I did not say anything to him at the time, as I did not want him to think I was skeptical of supernatural manifestations. I decided to do what the Scripture advises, "Test all things; hold fast what is good" (I Thes. 5:21).

Then a tragic thing happened. The evangelist, his wife and another girl were involved in a serious automobile accident. The girl was killed instantly, and the wife, barely escaping with her life, was completely paralyzed from her waist down. We were all shocked by the accident and sincerely hoped for the lady's full recovery.

The evangelist seemed confident that his wife would be healed. He confided to us that the miracle would be of such a startling nature that it would astonish the Church. Nevertheless, the months dragged by, and the woman did not receive deliverance. Apparently, the nerves of the spinal column had been severed and nothing short of a creative miracle would restore the woman to a normal condition.

At this time, I received a letter from this evangelist. He related a vision he had in which the "Angel Gabriel" talked to him about his wife's healing. According to him, the angel had informed him of the very day she was to be healed! Accordingly, he had made arrangements for photographers to be present at the time.

To me, the elements of the story did not ring true. The evangelist apparently sincerely believed in the "revelation" he had received. But the fact that the date was set and photographers were to be alerted seemed to me an ominous sign. The following was the pertinent part of his letter:

I have some news for you — I do believe it is directly from heaven. I've never written a letter like this before. I'm positive it is the hand of God. The Lord has shown me many wonderful things about our future ministry — auditoriums packed with tens of thousands — the greatest revivals I have ever seen or heard about ... .

On the morning of October 31, 1951, at about 5 a.m., I had a marvelous revelation. I was caught up into the heavens. Among the things I heard was my wife walking, and I heard the date of her miracle healing. I'm not to tell anyone according to the words spoken, only that the miracle will definitely be this fall. You remember I told you the Angel Gabriel came to me a week or so before the accident. Gabriel told me he would return at the appointed time. My wife will walk and preach again.

I am writing you a sealed letter. I know you will not open it as it contains the date of her healing. ... I wrote you and no one else knows of this date, and I'll phone you the hour she walks! I'll have cameras ready and get pictures. ... I know this will be a great stir and a victory for God.

When I received this letter, I had a feeling that he was receiving communications from seducing spirits — that he was so under their influence that nothing could be done to warn him. All I could do was to wait until the deception became evident. Several months passed, and as I did not hear anything, I finally opened the sealed letter which I discovered had been notarized. In the letter were the words:

I was caught up into the heavens and saw visions of God. At that time, a voice spoke to my anxious soul and told me the exact date of my wife's miracle recovery. The very date of her healing will be Nov. 24, 1951. ... She will walk in just 16 days from today. ... As I received the great heavenly vision, I saw my dear wife walking for the first time in nearly 2½ years. She was with me in revivals and standing beside me in the pulpit — her paralyzed body and nerves well again.

The date had come and gone, and of course nothing happened. This should have been a warning to the evangelist that he was being deceived. There was no excuse for him not to be on the alert. But was this the case? No! He was open for more "revelations" of an even more deceitful and unscriptural kind.

Some months afterward, news reached us that an "angel" had come again, and this time told him that the reason his "dear wife" was not healed was because she was not right with God. He was informed that if he divorced her and married another, then the blessing of God would again be upon his ministry. And that is exactly what this foolish evangelist did.

After that, he was no longer in active national ministry. Now and then we heard word that he attempted a meeting in this city and that. But his past soon caught up with him. Because of his inexcusable act — leaving his poor invalid wife to take care of herself and be an object of charity — most doors permanently closed to him. Such is the fruit of turning one's back on the plain statements of Scripture and giving heed to seducing spirits.

> But even if we, or an angel from heaven, preach any other gospel to you than what we have preached to you, let him be accursed (Gal. 1:8).

Case V — John Alexander Dowie's Seduction

During John Alexander Dowie's great healing ministry, a man came to him and told him that he (Dowie) was Elijah returned to earth. Dowie sharply rebuked him for suggesting such a thing and declared that a lying spirit had told him this. But Dowie never completely rid himself of the idea. He dallied with the thought, speculating whether he might be Elijah after all.

In time, the lying spirits impressed it so on his consciousness that the idea became more than a possibility; it turned into an obsession. He wanted to believe it, and the time finally came that he did. Thus Satan was able to destroy a great ministry. The man who had by his great faith brought deliverance to multitudes and had won the respect of the nation, suddenly, by his act of folly, destroyed his ministry and made himself the laughing stock of unbelievers.

A similar instance took place in recent years with another man of God. Fawning followers, anxious to bask in the light of a man greatly used of God, insisted that he was Elijah returned to earth. When he reluctantly went along with these people who were possessed by lying spirits, his ministry came to an abrupt end.

Lying spirits and seducing spirits are very similar in their operation. Seducing spirits are particularly characterized by their work of subverting people from the pure faith of the Gospel into some kind of perversion of it.

Case VI — Peter Hurkos' "Special Gift"

A serious accident can result in a broken arm or leg, or a concussion of the brain. A concussion may open the door to malicious spirits — familiar spirits, seducing spirits, insane spirits, spirits of divination, etc. And this has happened in not a few instances. We will take space to describe one, that of Peter Hurkos, who describes himself as a "psychometrist," and who is internationally known.

Mr. Hurkos said that before his accident he had no special gifts nor spiritual tendencies: "Our family had no religion at all and to the best of my knowledge, no one in our family had ever gone to church."

During the Hitler occupation, Hurkos was a member of the Dutch underground. While he was painting a barrack on a ladder, he lost his balance and fell 30 feet to the ground. Seriously injured by the fall, he was taken to the hospital, where he lay unconscious for several days.

When he awoke, he found that he had a severe skull fracture. The same day, he also discovered that he had a "new gift." He says,

"I did not know what it was at first, but I knew that suddenly I had a strange insight into the affairs of other people." He told the man lying next to him that he was a "bad" man for doing certain things. "It was not really I who told him he was a bad man, for even as I spoke the words, *I knew they were not my own, but those of a powerful being inside of me."* A demon spirit had entered into him. Hurkos further explains, "My own life was becoming a nightmare. Sometimes I thought I was crazy; at other times I wished I were. I did not want to pry into the private lives of others, but I was given no choice at all ... the pictures were there almost constantly, and they distracted me completely. Before my fall, I had never had such visions. But after this fall, my life was changed."

Hurkos sought after God, but his family were atheists. His mother thought he had gone out of his mind when he bought a Bible. There was no one to help him. Since he was so distracted by these visions, he couldn't work, but he found out that he could tell fortunes. He noted that the gift had no moral aspect, true of demonic revelations. It could be used to rob people or to gamble.

Hurkos had a spirit of divination. He was never released from it. He made his living telling fortunes with this demonic power, as did the girl in Acts 16:16. Hurkos was not a man of guile, but gave an honest account of the circumstances pertaining to the operation of his ability to read the human mind. As he grew older, his memory faded, and he became more and more a slave to his "gift."

Case VII — A Woman's Deliverance From Insanity

Many people have been set free in God-anointed song services from actual demon possession without any special prayer being made. Charles G. Finney, who lived before the apostolic outpouring of this century, tells of a marvelous deliverance of an insane woman in his meetings:

> There were two very striking cases of instantaneous recovery from insanity during this revival. As I went into the meeting in the afternoon of one Sabbath, I saw

several ladies sitting in a pew with a woman dressed in black, who seemed to be in great distress of mind; they were partly holding her and preventing her from going out. As I came in, one of the ladies came to me and told me that she was an insane woman. I said a few words to her; but she said she must go; and that she could not bear any praying or preaching or singing; that hell was her portion; and she could not endure anything that made her think of heaven.

I cautioned the ladies privately to keep her in her seat, if they could, without disturbing the meeting. As soon as the singing began, she struggled hard to get out. But the ladies obstructed her passage and kindly but persistently prevented her escape. After a few moments, she became quiet, but seemed to avoid hearing or attending to all the singing. I then prayed. The Lord gave me a great spirit of prayer and a text from Hebrews: "Let us therefore come boldly unto the throne of grace, that we may obtain mercy, and find grace to help in time of need" (4:16 KJV).

My object was to encourage faith in ourselves and in her, and in ourselves for her. As I proceeded, she began gradually to raise her head and look at me from within her long black bonnet. As I proceeded to urge the people to be bold in their faith, to launch out and commit themselves with utmost confidence to God through the atoning sacrifice of our great High Priest, all at once she startled the congregation by uttering a loud shriek. She then cast herself almost from her seat, held her head very low, and I could see that she "trembled very exceedingly." As I proceeded she began to look up again, and soon sat upright with face wonderfully changed, indicating triumphant joy and peace. There was such a glow upon her countenance as I have seldom seen in any human face. Her joy was so great that she could scarcely contain herself till the meeting was over; and then she soon made everybody understand around her that she was at liberty. She glorified God and rejoiced with amazing triumph. About two years later, I met with her and found her still full of joy and peace.

Case VIII — John Smith's Deliverance From Insanity

One of the most remarkable deliverances from insane demons is the case of a friend of mine. Just after his marriage, he had a nervous breakdown — a circumstance that invites demon possession.

Previous to his mental collapse, he developed a spirit of restlessness. Wherever he was, he wanted to be somewhere else. He had a sharp temper, and it got more and more out of control. He would beat his wife, and then in sudden fits of temper, he would beat the walls of the house, or kick the doors until the panels were splintered. His wife witnessed his mental breakdown with tears and apprehension.

A spirit of jealousy took control of him, and he accused his wife of unfaithfulness though she had been altogether true to him. A babble of voices tormented him. It was a case of paranoic schizophrenia — or demon possession.

Finally, his case got so bad that he was committed to an asylum. There he became so violent that he had to be strapped on a bed. Of his condition he later testified, "My mind was so confused and seemed to be split in two, so that I could not think straight. I lived in a fantasy world of my own, and I cannot tell you of the awful horrible delusions I had. I fought the attendants who came to shave me, as I was convinced they were cutting my throat. I laughed madly. I was just stark insane!"

His wife was advised that her husband was doomed to spend his life in an asylum, and that she should get a divorce. Instead she began to pray for his deliverance. She heard of two men who were praying for the sick. She wrote a letter to them of her husband's condition. Would these brethren come and see him? These men had faith in God. They went to the asylum and after being given permission to visit my friend, they laid hands on him and rebuked the demons in the Name of the Lord Jesus Christ.

Something really happened! The power of God flashed, and the demons went out. My friend tells what happened: "The glory of God filled my soul, and a great light fell on me, like the noon-day sun, and I jumped up crying, 'I am healed,' while tears streamed down my face. Rest came to my mind and soul. Confidence returned to my being, and I knew I was touched by the almighty skilled Physician, who never lost a case."

Like the demoniac in the Scriptures, he told the story of his deliverance everywhere. He was called into the ministry and has been preaching many years. Not long ago I saw him, and he was still praising God for His great mercy.

Case IX — The Danger of Trifling With Demons

Demons are nothing to trifle with. I recall the case of a man and a woman who came to one of our meetings in a rather frivolous frame of mind. They were accustomed to services in which there was a great deal of noise and commotion, including jumping and screaming. The service had been an impressive one in which many deaf and mute spirits had been cast out, but all of this meant nothing to them because it was not like the services they were used to. They came afterward and told me that there was no real power in the service. They were quite dogmatic in their attitude, and as I tried to explain matters to them, I perceived I was making no headway.

Suddenly during our conversation, the lady began to shake and tremble. At first, the husband thought his wife was under the power of God. But he soon learned otherwise. Apparently one of the evil spirits that had just been cast out, noting her contentious and irreverent spirit, took possession of her. Soon the couple was in a panic. I took the two to a private room in the rear, and I told the lady that we were going to cast out this spirit in the Name of Jesus, but first she must promise that she would never again be irreverent in the house of the Lord. Both she and her husband were glad to make the promise, and the woman was immediately delivered.

Human pride causes some people to rush boldly in where angels fear to tread. A brilliant young lady evangelist told me some years ago of a very painful experience she had. At that time, some of the evangelists who worked with us were having campaigns with very large attendance in which divine healing was emphasized and demonstrated. The young lady had been quite successful in her ministry until that time, and confessed she was jealous that suddenly these campaigns were taking the spotlight. She determined that she too was to pray for the sick.

Now her resolution was quite all right, but in dealing with sick people and especially those who are demon possessed, certain precautions are necessary. One can be a great orator or a brilliant musician able to hold the attention of a crowd due to natural talents. But in ministering to those sorely afflicted by Satan, such as those under the control of demons, an anointing of the Spirit is necessary that comes only as a result of waiting upon God. This may mean days of prayer and sometimes fasting, as indicated by the words of Jesus.

About that time, some people in the church where she was holding a campaign told her of an insane woman in the neighborhood. Would she kindly come and pray for the woman? The evangelist told them she would. The lady indeed was in a serious condition, and there was no doubt that it was a case of demon possession.

Without further ado, the evangelist laid her hands upon the woman and commanded the evil spirit to come out. The woman was instantly delivered, *but the demon entered into the evangelist.* Her first realization that something serious had happened was that she began to shake violently. She could not rid herself of the condition, and found that her mind was being taken over by another entity. An overwhelming sense of despair seized her as she realized that the exorcised demon or demons had entered into her. Of course, she could not continue the campaign, and her condition soon became so grave that her relatives had to commit her to an asylum.

Now there is something for those who believe they are wise in these things to ponder. Here was a young lady, a successful soul-winner, suddenly possessed of evil spirits. How could this have happened to a saved person, much less to a minister of the Gospel? In answering this question, we must understand that a human being is triune: body, soul and spirit. Devils are able to afflict the bodies of believers, as is proven both by Scripture (Job 2:7; Lk. 13:16) and also by common observation. The promises of God give the believer authority over Satan's power. But they have to be appropriated, and Satan's minions are not bashful at all in usurping the believer's rights wherever and whenever they are not resisted and put in their place. "Resist the devil and he will flee from you" (Jas. 4:7), is more than a slogan; it is a command.

It is pitifully clear that Satan steals the rights of many a believer. How few claim the blessing of Psalm 91! Read it through carefully before an answer is given. Alas, the devil can oppress the body of a saint and afflict him if he does not take scriptural precautions, and in some cases, can enter even into the realm of a person's mind. Nevertheless, there is a limit to which the devil can go. He cannot cross the bloodline of a blood-washed saint.

Now this young lady knew she was in a bad way. She could not control her thoughts, but she was aware that the demons had lodged in her mind and were responsible for her condition. No one she knew seemed to have the power to believe for her deliverance, and she had to rely upon her own faith. All she could think of were the words of Jesus, "This kind goeth not out but by prayer and fasting" (Matt. 17:21 KJV).

But how could she fast? Attendants brought her meals every day, and they would immediately notice if her food lay untouched. If she couldn't pray, she could at least fast, but how could she do it unobserved? She solved this by disposing of her food through the plumbing when attendants were not watching. This went on for weeks, with no one being the wiser.

However, one cannot fast indefinitely without losing weight, and of course, this became noticeable in time. When the situation was finally discovered, attendants forced food into her stomach.

No sooner were the attendants gone than a reaction set in. The young woman threw up all the food, but even as this severe physical reaction took place, the demons went out too! Her mind suddenly had become clear and calm, and she knew she was delivered. A short time later, her brother came and took her away from the institution. Soon, her health fully restored, she returned to the ministry.

There is not the slightest doubt that this woman's soul was covered the whole time by the blood. Nevertheless, she had involved herself in a battle with powerful demons with which she was not prepared to cope. It was a frightening experience to her, but in the end a profitable one, for she knew what it was to war against dark powers. And that is why the Apostle Paul in Ephesians 6 warns us to take the full armor of God in our warfare against the spirits of wickedness (Eph. 6:12-18).

Case X — The Demon-Possessed Intruder

One of the cases in which a man under demonic control attempted a daring confrontation with a man of God in a public assembly occurred some years ago in the city auditorium in Portland, Oregon. The incident happened during a campaign which the writer was managing. Early in the service, just as the evangelist had begun to speak, a man walked up the aisle onto the platform with a menacing attitude. In a loud voice, he began to denounce the minister, cursing him, calling him a snake in the grass, a deceiver of the people, a liar. It was an obvious case of demon possession.

The disturbance threw a momentary scare into the ministers, a large number of whom were sitting on the platform. The challenger was strong physically and well able to carry out his threats against the diminutive evangelist. However, the man of God went over and stood beside him and began to take dominion over him in the Name of Jesus, saying, "Satan, because you have come here to cast reproach on the man of God and to harm the Lord's anointed, therefore, in the Name of Jesus, you must fall down before me on the floor." The man suddenly began to be under a terrible strain; his eyes bulged, his veins stood out, beads of perspiration stood on his forehead as he ineffectually tried to withstand the power that was overcoming him. Suddenly, with a groan, he fell to the floor, sobbing. Satan had met his match.

But the man was not fully delivered since he did not desire deliverance from the demon. We learned afterward, he had broken up services in various churches previously, but there was no one with the faith to deal with him. So far as we know, he never again repeated his performance.

Case XI — The Believers' Power Over the Enemy

> Then the seventy returned with joy, saying, "Lord, even the demons are subject to us in Your name." And He said to them, "I saw Satan fall like lightning from heaven. Behold, I give you the authority to trample on serpents and scorpions, and over all the power of the enemy, and nothing shall by any means hurt you" (Lk. 10:17-19).

An instance of the casting out of an insane demon from the book, *The New John G. Lake Sermons*, relates the power of the believer over demons. The story of this remarkable deliverance took place in South Africa. Dr. Lake begins by telling of the conversion of a young man named Von Shield. After he received the baptism of the Spirit, Von Shield retired to the mountains to pray. When he returned weeks later, he had received a mighty anointing of the Spirit. Dr. Lake tells what happened:

> One day he (Von Shield) returned under such an anointing of the Spirit as I have never before witnessed on any life. Not long after that he came to me and said, "Brother Lake, did you know this was in the Bible?" And he proceeded to read to me that familiar verse in the 16th chapter of Mark: "These signs shall follow them that believe; In my name shall they cast out devils." Looking up into my face with great earnestness, he said, "My! I wish I knew somebody that had a devil!"
>
> I believe God had planned that situation, for I was

reminded that in my mail a couple of days before had come a request for an insane son. The mother said, "As far as I can tell my son has a devil," and her request was that we might come and pray that the devil might be cast out. He said, "Why this is only a couple or three blocks from where I live. I am going to find this fellow and then I am coming back for you."

I said to myself, "Here is a newborn soul, whose vision enters into the real realm of God-power." I realized that my own spirit had not touched the degree of faith that was in that soul, and I said to myself, "I do not want to say a word or do a thing that will discourage that soul in the least."

Presently he came back and said, "Brother Lake, come on." We went and found a boy who had been mad from his birth; he was like a wild animal. He would not wear clothes and would smash himself or anybody else with anything that was given him. He couldn't even have a dish to eat on. But in the center of the enclosure where he was they had a large stone hollowed out and they would put his food in that and let him eat it just like an animal.

We tried to catch him, but he was wild as a lion. He would jump right over my head. Finally his father said, "You will not catch him out there." I had been somewhat of an athlete in my youth and I said to Von Shield, "You get on one side and if he comes to your side you will take care of him, and if he comes to my side I will take care of him."

Now beloved, this all sounds strange I know, but I'll never forget that afternoon as long as I live. As I looked to that young man I could see the lightning flash of faith, and I knew that if he got his hands on that man that devil would come out.

Presently he landed on my side of the bed, and in an instant Von Shield sprang over the bed, laid his hands on his head and commanded the devil to come out. In two minutes that man was absolutely transformed, and was a sane man, the first moment of sanity he ever knew.

Chapter Fourteen

Spiritualism

Spiritualism is real, just as Satan is real. We know that the devil exists and that he is never up to any good. Although much that goes on in spiritualism is fraud and trickery, some of the phenomena manifested in the séance room is genuine. The source of the manifestation is demonic rather than human. Nearly all the kinds of sorcery and black magic practiced during Bible days are being repeated again today.

Usually the manifestation of spiritual phenomena requires the presence of a medium with "psychic powers," which is actually the working of what the Bible calls a familiar demonic spirit. However, mediums often find that regular séances are extremely trying, and in time, they are apt to resort to trickery and deception rather than submit themselves to demon spirits. They can secure the same effects through sleight of hand, and it is easier than going into a trance.

Investigators of spiritualism have discovered so much trickery among its practitioners that some of them have come to the conclusion that it is *all* sleight of hand. However, they are mistaken. Today there are some genuine manifestations of preternatural phenomena, though the supposed communication with the dead is actually the work of deceiving spirits that simulate the voice and personality of the person they are impersonating.

In this chapter, we will briefly discuss various common spirit phenomena manifested in spiritualistic séances or elsewhere. This is important to understand, for this communication with evil spirits is actually the same as the sorcery recorded in the Bible. Not understanding these things, some people assume everything supernatural is of God. They mistake what is actually sorcery to be the power of God, as the people in Philip's day did (Acts 8:9-11).

The Ouija Board

Ouija boards became popular during World War I, when so many people lost loved ones. The Ouija board is just one apparatus used by novices to obtain spirit messages. Users are encouraged to yield to the "universal psychic powers." If they are properly in tune, the pointer will dance around on the numbers and alphabet, spelling out words. Usually nothing but garbled gibberish is received; however, on occasion, intelligible messages appear. In such cases, the messages don't come from the dead, but from impersonating demon spirits.

Spirit Photographs

Many of the photographs supposedly produced by mediums are plain fakes. Sometimes the demonstration will include "paintings" supposedly done on the spot. Mediums present an ordinary blank canvas for inspection. Then without completely removing it from the sight of the person, an oil painting is produced which appears to have been done so recently that the paint is still wet. In most cases, the painting was there all the time with a blank canvas over it. The medium diverts the attention of the client and cleverly removes the blank canvas. Rubbing a little poppy oil on the painting makes it appear freshly painted.

Despite these patent frauds, there are apparently some genuine photographs which cannot be explained by natural means. Sir Conan Doyle, the famous scientist and author of *Sherlock Holmes*, after using every scientific precaution, became convinced that certain mediums are able to produce genuine spirit photographs by supernatural methods. Doyle later became a patron of spiritualism. Again, seducing spirits are responsible.

Communication With the Dead

By far the most popular and most widely known practice of spiritualism is the pretense of communication with the dead. This practice has led many who are ignorant of the Scriptures astray. The Bible condemns this practice in the severest terms. One of the first commands in the Mosaic Law to Israel was: "You shall not permit a sorceress (a medium) to live" (Ex. 22:18). Elsewhere in the Old Testament, serious warnings are given about seeking advice from the dead through consulting mediums.

> And when they say to you, "Seek those who are mediums and wizards, who whisper and mutter," should not a people seek their God? *Should they seek* the dead on behalf of the living? (Isa. 8:19).

The clearest warning against this practice is found in the story of Saul when he sought counsel from Samuel through the witch of En Dor. This account was put in the Bible to expose the fraudulence of spiritualism. During the early years of his reign, Saul had banished those who dealt with familiar spirits (I Sam. 28:3). But toward the end of Saul's career, because of his backslidden condition, everything was going against him. He no longer received any word from God, and he became desperate. With the Philistines coming against him, and the prospect of defeat apparently certain, he decided to consult a witch.

Upon inquiry, a woman with a familiar spirit was discovered at En Dor. Disguising himself, Saul and two companions went to the witch's cave in the nearby mountains to seek her counsel. The cave was dimly lighted, and the medium did not immediately recognize her visitors. She had strong misgivings when she realized what they wanted, having been forbidden previously by Saul to ply her trade on pain of death. The king reassured her on oath that no harm would come to her, and so she was persuaded to make the attempt to "bring up Samuel" (I Sam. 28:11) for her visitors.

The woman went into a trance. The impersonating spirits in the séance can be so subtle that the very intonations of the voice of the departed person are perfectly simulated. In most cases, messages are supposedly given from a departed loved one. When a message comes through, usually the inquirer is too excited to check its authenticity.

William S. Sadler has investigated spiritualism extensively. In his book, he shows the fraudulence of these communications:

> Again and again have I tried through mediums, when supposedly in communication with some deceased scholar, to get the spirit to dictate to the medium something pertaining to the spirit's professional specialties when they were on earth. For instance, I have a deceased friend who was a physician and a very dear friend. In my investigation of spiritism, I have supposedly been in communication with this physician many times, but never have I been able to get the spirit to quote some passage from some medical authority that I might suggest. Never could I get the medium to spell out medical terms properly, never could I get the medium to name the diagnosis we made of a certain case which we had in consultation or to cite the authorities investigated at that conference which led to the making of the diagnosis. In a score of ways, I have given these mediums an opportunity to prove that they were in communication with bona fide discarnate spirits, but in every instance they have wholly and completely — yes, dismally — failed.
>
> I have talked with George Washington, Abraham Lincoln, Thomas Paine, Socrates, Plato, Milton and other of the great minds of past ages, but in no case have I ever secured from mediums anything from these old masters that would bear the least semblance to the product of their minds when living on earth — and mind you, I communicated with them with reference to the very things they thought about and discussed when living. I did not ask questions pertaining to their present state in

the spirit world. I did not ask for a description of the landscape and geography of spiritland. I asked them about the very things they authoritatively discussed when living, and they unfailingly defaulted in their efforts to show any degree of familiarity with those subjects in which they were specialists in life.

Hodgson, Myers and others have left sealed messages, written in cipher, and so far no medium has ever been able to interpret them; no one has ever approached an interpretation of these code messages. But so far, that test has failed every time.

If we could call up the spirits of the departed, and they were really true to their professed identity, we might hear something worthwhile. As someone suggested not long since, it would be interesting to get Isaac Newton on the wire and hear what he thought of the Einstein theory of relativity. We would likewise be glad to hear from George Washington on the League of Nations, what Gladstone thought about the Irish Treaty, or from Abraham Lincoln on the Four-Power Naval Pact. It would be interesting to hear what Alexander the Great might have thought of the military strategy at Verdun. But strange to say, when the mediums do bring out these dignitaries and sages of a past age, they are much more likely to talk about substitutes for coffee, removable dental bridges, or to discuss some other trifle, the purport of which is to try and convince those present that spirits are real because they can tell you about something you have lost or which has been stolen, etc. The whole business is too trivial and juvenile to be worthy of the serious attention of sober-minded, thinking men and women.

There was a Jewish fellow who went to consult a medium, and she told him his mother was present. He talked with his mother's spirit, and she gave him messages from

> other relatives who had passed over, and at the end, the medium asked if there were any other questions he would like to ask his mother, and he said: "You know Mother, we used to have such nice visits in Hebrew, and now if I could just have a little talk with you in Yiddish, then I'd know it was you." But the ghost could not talk Yiddish.

Now back to Saul and the witch of En Dor. The usual procedure of the séance was, in this case, cut short. In this one and only instance, it appears that God permitted the real person (Samuel) to speak. The woman realized that the one speaking was not her usual "control spirit" at all. It was apparently the real Samuel, who delivered a most solemn rebuke to the ill-fated king.

> Now Samuel said to Saul, "Why have you disturbed me by bringing me up?" And Saul answered, "I am deeply distressed; for the Philistines make war against me, and God has departed from me and does not answer me anymore, neither by prophets nor by dreams. Therefore I have called you, that you may reveal to me what I should do." Then Samuel said: "So why do you ask me, seeing the LORD has departed from you and has become your enemy? And the LORD has done for Himself as He spoke by me. For the LORD has torn the kingdom out of your hand and given it to your neighbor, David. ... Moreover the LORD will also deliver Israel with you into the hand of the Philistines. And tomorrow you and your sons *will be* with me. The LORD will also deliver the army of Israel into the hand of the Philistines" (I Sam. 28:15-17,19).

The familiar spirit of the woman was apparently not a factor at all in bringing up Samuel. God took the matter out of the devil's hands. Familiar spirits may *impersonate* the dead, but they cannot *produce* the dead. This is the only case in the Bible where God allowed a man to communicate with a person who was dead. And then it was allowed only to condemn the proceedings and pronounce judgment on the one who had sought such counsel. Most alleged spirit communications are expressed in terms that will leave a favorable impression. But Samuel rebuked the inquirer sternly. In the case of the rich man and Lazarus (Lk. 16:29-31), the departed rich man begged Abraham to permit Lazarus to go and warn his five brethren not to come to where he was. But his petition was denied. It was not God's plan. Abraham said that if people will not repent in response to the warnings in the Scripture, they would not repent even if someone rose from the dead. To play with spiritism is direct disobedience to the command of Scripture and is an invitation for demons to come and make their abode there.

Materialization — Sorcery

According to the theory of spiritualism, the spirit of a human being can, under certain circumstances, leave the body. According to spiritists, the spirit must keep some contact with the body, at least by a slender thread; otherwise the person dies. Some professional mediums apparently have power, with the assistance of demon power, to actually materialize an object or move objects without physical contact. In most cases, that which is materialized has no permanent existence in the natural world and soon dissipates. This is purely sorcery — a practice that the Bible warns against. Many such "signs, and lying wonders" (II Thes. 2:9) will appear at the end time, and God's people must be alert.

When God creates, His creation remains. Sorcery materializes things and then dematerializes them. The oil made by God through Elijah and Elisha remained given for useful purposes. The serpents that appeared as the result of the Egyptian sorcerers' art were swallowed up by Aaron's rod. The substances and illusions found in spiritualism work best in the darkness of the séance and usually vanish before critical examination.

The Word of God gives dire warnings against sorcery, witchcraft, wizardry and all kinds of black magic. Those who tamper with dark powers do so at extreme peril to their own souls. As we have said,

Scripture gives full information concerning the state of the departed dead, and there is no need for anyone to seek guidance from familiar spirits. In the first place, their information would be false. Secondly, the seeker would very likely be lured into bondage to evil spirits. Spiritualism is one of Satan's greatest deceptions and most potent means of bringing people under the influence and control of demons.

Chapter Fifteen

Discerning Evil Spirits

Beloved, do not believe every spirit, but test the spirits, whether they are of God; because many false prophets have gone out into the world (I Jn. 4:1).

How can we discern the presence or the operation of evil spirits? How can we distinguish evil manifestations from those of the Spirit of God? There are times when it is not easy to identify what is divine and what is not, as in the case of Aaron's rod and the magicians' rods. The Scriptures give us a number of methods by which the test can be made. There is no need for anyone to be confused if he is willing to take time to learn what the Word of God has to say on the matter.

Test I — Does the Evil Spirit Deny Any Part of the Word of God?

For the first test, let us go back to the tragic story of Eve in the Garden of Eden. She foolishly allowed herself to be deceived by Satan, who had embodied himself in the serpent. Had she realized that this was her archenemy, Satan, who was seeking her ruin, she would have fled from him in terror. But she did not, and she yielded to his subtle suggestion. Later, she discovered her terrible mistake.

The penalty for this mistake staggers the imagination. What did Eve neglect to do that might have saved her from such a tragic error? Eve's first mistake was being near the prohibited tree. She put herself in a position where she could become a victim of temptation. She must have realized she was probably doing wrong. Multitudes are like Eve; they deliberately go where temptation is. They play with fire, naively thinking they will not be burned. Today people insist on dabbling in all sorts of black arts and mysticism, and it is not surprising that many of them become entangled in it.

Eve's greatest mistake was doubting the veracity of God's Word. The Lord had said, "In the day that you eat of it you shall surely die" (Gen. 2:17). The serpent insinuated that Eve was foolish to believe this. He did not come right out and call God a liar, but he raised questions in Eve's mind. "Has God indeed said?" (Gen. 3:1). That insidious suggestion should have been enough to cause Eve to flee from her enemy. The devil is a liar by nature. Sooner or later, though he appears in sheep's clothing, he will inevitably reveal the cloven hoof by casting doubt on the Word of God. Yet, often people allow themselves, like Eve did, to be led on into serious delusion because they consider the devil's suggestions rather than hold to the Word of God!

Earlier we cited the instance of an evangelist who was led astray through seducing spirits. These spirits had told him that on a given day, a spectacular healing miracle was going to take place in his paralyzed wife — a healing that would attract national attention. When this prophecy failed to come to pass, the spirits then told him that the miracle could not take place because his wife was out of the will of God and that he must divorce his wife and marry another. Then his ministry would be crowned with success. The minister chose to believe the seducing spirit rather than the Word of God. When his words did not come to pass, this man should have recognized that he was possessed of a lying spirit.

The test of a true prophet is given in Deuteronomy 18:21,22:

> And if you say in your heart, "How shall we know the word which the LORD has not spoken?" — when a prophet speaks in the name of the LORD, if the thing does not happen or come to pass, that *is* the thing which the LORD has not spoken; the prophet has spoken it

presumptuously; you shall not be afraid of him.

A seducing spirit can usually be detected because its nature is to lie and to make statements in direct contradiction to the Word of God. However, if the person has allowed himself to come under the influence of a lying spirit, he is in grave danger of rationalizing the lies rather than believing the Word of God.

Sometimes Christians are led astray when they are told by a lying spirit that God has honored them by giving them a "new revelation." If they choose to believe the seducing spirit rather than the Word of God, their usefulness as a Christian is ended, or at least diminished. Indeed, their soul may actually be in peril.

Test II — Does the Evil Spirit Deny Christ Has Come in the Flesh?

By this you know the Spirit of God: Every spirit that confesses that Jesus Christ has come in the flesh is of God, and every spirit that does not confess that Jesus Christ has come in the flesh is not of God. And this is the *spirit* of the Antichrist, which you have heard was coming, and is now already in the world (I Jn. 4:2,3).

This is not so much a test of an evil spirit, but a test of whether a prophet or teacher is being influenced by a seducing spirit introducing some new doctrine or cult. The spirit behind false religion will usually cause a human leader to contradict or distort the truth of Christ's deity. In other words, the teaching will generally deny or throw doubt in some way upon the fact that Jesus was born of a virgin and is the Son of God. Islam, for instance, concedes that Jesus was a prophet, but only in the sense that Mohammed was a prophet.

There are a dozen or so cults familiar to the public which in some way or another fall into the category referred to in I John 4:1-3. Invariably, their teachings strike at the most vital point of the Gospel: the deity of Jesus Christ.

One cult that emphasizes mental healing denies that the physical universe exists at all. They claim that all is spirit, and therefore there is no actual physical body. Consequently, there can be no actual sickness, pain or death. Such a philosophy of course must deny that Jesus came in the *flesh*, that He *suffered* on the cross and died, and that He arose again in a glorified *body*. Large numbers of people have fallen into the delusion of this cult. Had they carefully read the New Testament, they would never have become a victim of such an error.

Other cults teach that Jesus of Nazareth came in the flesh, but they do not believe that He was the Christ, the Son of God. The acid test of all doctrine is whether it accepts the fundamental truth that Jesus is the Christ. Without equivocation, all teachers who are of God will make the same confession Peter did when Jesus asked him, "But who do you say that I am?" (Matt. 16:15).

> Simon Peter answered and said, "You are the Christ, the Son of the living God" (Matt. 16:16).

Another well-known cult teaches that Jesus was only a created being, like other men. It maintains that because He faithfully obeyed the commandments of God, He became the Anointed One of God, and in that sense, He was the Son of God. This is false. Christ is not a created being, but the eternal Son of God, Who through the incarnation also became the Son of Man.

The spirit behind modernism (devalues supernatural elements), unitarianism (believes that the deity exists only in one person), universalism (claims that all will be saved), New Thought (a mental movement devoted to the creative power of constructive thinking), and a score of other religions, in some way denies the divinity of Jesus Christ. Wherever doubt is expressed concerning this fundamental cornerstone of the Gospel, one may be certain that seducing spirits have been operating.

Test III — You Shall Know Them by Their Fruits

Is the power to perform miracles an infallible test of a person's standing with God? Is the fact that a person can speak with languages of men and even of angels proof that he has the true Spirit? If an individual preaches inspired messages, is that in itself proof that he is right with God? If someone was once anointed of God, is it certain that he or she now has the Spirit of Christ? I Corinthians 13:1-3 has something to say about this:

> Though I speak with the tongues of men and of angels, but have not love, I have become sounding brass or a clanging cymbal. And though I have *the gift of* prophecy, and understand all mysteries and all knowledge, and though I have all faith, so that I could remove mountains, but have not love, I am nothing. And though I bestow all my goods to feed *the poor,* and though I give my body to be burned, but have not love, it profits me nothing.

Ordinarily, if a person operates in the divine gifts, it is because he or she is anointed of God. But the gifts are not infallible signs, because unfortunately, those who possess them are free moral agents and may yield to self-exaltation and, as Paul declares, become "false apostles" (II Cor. 11:13). The love of money may cause a person to err like Judas, one of the Twelve. He performed miracles, but in the end because he was a traitor, he betrayed his Master for 30 pieces of silver. Samson was anointed of God, but he yielded to fleshly lusts and eventually was deprived of his power and fell into the snare of the enemy (Judg. 16:20,21).

Balaam spoke some beautiful prophecies; he even prophesied of the coming of Christ (Num. 24:17). But because of his love of money, Balaam commercialized his gift and in the end, died under the judgment of God (Josh. 13:22).

Jesus gave a grave warning concerning these things in Matthew 7:22,23:

> Many will say to Me in that day, "Lord, Lord, have we not prophesied in Your name, cast out demons in Your name, and done many wonders in Your name?" And then I will declare to them, "I never knew you; depart from Me, you who practice lawlessness!"

What then is the true test of the prophet of God? Jesus gave it when He said:

> Every tree that does not bear good fruit is cut down and thrown into the fire. Therefore by their fruits you will know them (Matt. 7:19,20).

How do we judge a prophet who claims to be sent of God and who backs up his claims with signs like casting a rod on the ground and causing it to turn into a serpent? Remember that the magicians, as well as Moses and Aaron, had power to turn their rods into serpents. So how can we distinguish between what is of God and what is of the devil, when the signs appear the same?

Before we answer that question, let us first ask some others. Does the one claiming to be of God possess the same spirit of humility Moses had? "Now the man Moses *was* very humble, more than all men who *were* on the face of the earth" (Num. 12:3). Is the person an intercessor of Moses' caliber, willing to give his life for the salvation of his people? Does he or she fight and beat the people of God, like Pharaoh's servants did? If a person exudes the fruit of the Spirit, we can then judge his signs as being of God. On the other hand, if the individual seeks self-aggrandizement like Pharaoh did or plays with sorcery like the magicians did, he or she must be counted on the side of Satan.

Sorcerers are often able to perform a materialization, but it will have no permanent existence in the world. Aaron's rod remained, but the serpents of the magicians were swallowed up. When spiritists, on occasion, are able to cause solid objects to materialize, this is not the power of God, but sorcery. UFOs, which appear and disappear, fall into this category. When Elijah produced oil and meal, they lasted all during the famine to sustain the widow's family (I Ki. 17:14-16). When Elisha brought forth oil, it remained to pay the debts of the wife of one of the sons of the prophets (II Ki. 4:1-7). When Christ multiplied the loaves and fish, even the leftovers remained and were gathered up for future use (Matt. 15:32-37). The magicians of Pharaoh could produce serpents, but they vanished before the power of God! Spiritualism and religious sorcery can produce materializations, but they will eventually vanish. This is the mark of sorcery. Let the people of God beware!

Test IV — The Gift of Discernment

We have considered three tests for the "trying of spirits," which any Christian familiar with the Word of God may use. If these tests are applied carefully and prayerfully, it is inconceivable that a believer could be led away by any of Satan's delusions, however subtle. For all practical purposes, the Christian only needs these three tests to discern between the true and the false. However, there are those who function in areas of ministry that bring them into frequent contact with evil powers, and it is necessary that they be able to quickly identify evil powers at work — especially where more than one demon is present. For those times when it is needed, God has provided a special gift called the "discerning of spirits." This gift is mentioned in I Corinthians 12:7,8,10:

> But the manifestation of the Spirit is given to each one for the profit *of all*: for to one is given ... discerning of spirits.

Discerning of spirits is a gift of wider scope than is generally realized. There are evil spirits and good spirits. Sometimes God permits His people to discern the presence of good spirits. Elisha prayed that his servant would be able to see the protecting army of angels, and immediately his eyes were opened:

> And Elisha prayed, and said, "LORD, I pray, open his eyes that he may see." Then the LORD opened the eyes of the young man, and he saw. And behold, the mountain *was* full of horses and chariots of fire all around Elisha (II Ki. 6:17).

Discerning of spirits also allows believers to have discernment regarding human spirits. Philip, the evangelist, thinking Simon Magus was a true believer, baptized him in water. But when Peter came, he discerned that Simon was a sorcerer, and exposed him at once (Acts 8:9-23). Jesus knew that Judas was a hypocrite, although the latter cleverly hid his real character from the rest of the disciples (Matt. 26:21,22). Gehazi thought he had deceived Elisha concerning the talent of silver and the changes of raiment. But Elisha knew what his treacherous servant had done (II Ki. 5:20-27). The gift of discernment, however, is particularly designed to detect the presence of demons. On occasion, these spirits will pretend to be the Spirit of God, and thereby escape detection.

A particular trick that demons sometimes use is illustrated in the case of the slave girl who attended Paul's first campaign in Europe. This girl had a spirit of divination, and through her fortunetelling she brought her masters much financial gain. She followed Paul, crying out, "These men are the servants of the Most High God, who proclaim to us the way of salvation" (Acts 16:17).

Perhaps some of the followers of Paul supposed that the girl had the Spirit of God, and that what she said was a genuine testimony to the Lord Jesus Christ. Paul, however, discerned the presence of the divining spirit and recognized that her testimony was doing harm in identifying him with these practitioners of the black art and familiar spirits. Paul immediately cast out the evil spirit so that the girl was no longer able to harass him or tell the fortunes of those who visited him. Paul and Silas got thrown in prison for this, and God sent an earthquake to free them.

God has provided ample resources for believers so that no one need be deceived by seducing spirits. Unfortunately, many people fail to heed the scriptural warnings and use the tests of truth and error that God has given. Consequently, great numbers are being ensnared by false spirits, whose zeal to delude will continue to increase in these last days (I Tim. 4:1).

Part IV:

Demons and the Occult

Chapter Sixteen

Sorcery and Divination

There are so many forms of sorcery and divination that it would require considerable space to make even an approximate list. Under the general terms of sorcery and divination, there are many kinds of occult practices. These include augury (prognostications), the interpretation of signs and omens, astrology (a form of divination based on the belief that astral bodies direct the destinies of people), black and white magic, soothsaying, fortunetelling, the interpreting of dreams, the use of divining rods, etc. The list is very long.

Necromancy, or communication with the dead, is a specialized form of divination which has become quite popular today. Witchery and wizardry which traffic in familiar spirits are denounced in no uncertain terms in the Scriptures. These spirits feign to be the spirits of departed dead. They operate through a medium, which in the King James Version is properly called a witch.

Sorcery is a term that more or less includes the whole spectrum of psychic phenomena. Another term is witchcraft, which also involves demonic practices, especially those practiced among primitive tribes. The arts of witchery commonly include pronouncement of curses, casting of spells, destroying lives, upsetting nature and causing all kinds of calamities. Practitioners of witchcraft in foreign lands, contrary to those in America, usually do not deny that they are in league with demonic powers. Nevertheless, even in America in recent years there are those, like Anton Szander LaVey of the Satanist Church in San Francisco, who openly and with pride confess that their powers come from Satan.

Each form of sorcery differs in some way from others, but all operate through the activities of demons. On the whole, however, modern practitioners prefer to classify their art under the more respectable name of psychic research. Their operations include telepathy, automatic writing, trances, luminous apparitions, ESP, clairvoyance, clairaudience, written spirit communications, materializations, levitations, spirit-rapping, and others.

The Scriptures unequivocally denounce all these various forms of sorcery and divination. The Mosaic injunction in Leviticus 19:31 warns the people against these practices saying:

> Give no regard to mediums and familiar spirits; do not seek after them, to be defiled by them: I *am* the LORD your God.

Again the inspired writer says, "And the person who turns to mediums and familiar spirits, to prostitute himself with them, I will set My face against that person and cut him off from his people" (Lev. 20:6). Isaiah the prophet reproves the people who traffic with the spirits and says, "Should not a people seek their God? *Should they seek* the dead on behalf of the living?" (Isa. 8:19).

Demons not only operate outside of Christian circles, but whenever possible, they work inside the Church, as the Apostle Paul foretold. "Now the Spirit expressly says that in latter times some will depart from the faith, giving heed to deceiving spirits and doctrines of demons" (I Tim. 4:1). These spirits are responsible for the heresies that get into the church.

John sums up the warning against these seducing demons by saying:

> Beloved, do not believe every spirit, but test the spirits, whether they are of God; because many false prophets have gone out into the world. By this you know the Spirit of God: Every spirit that confesses that Jesus Christ has come in the flesh is of God, and every spirit that does not confess that Jesus Christ has come in the flesh is not

of God. And this is the *spirit* of the Antichrist, which you have heard was coming, and is now already in the world (I Jn. 4:1-3).

Spirits of Divination

Now it happened, as we went to prayer, that a certain slave girl possessed with a spirit of divination met us, who brought her masters much profit by fortune-telling. This girl followed Paul and us, and cried out, saying, "These men are the servants of the Most High God, who proclaim to us the way of salvation." And this she did for many days. But Paul, greatly annoyed, turned and said to the spirit, "I command you in the name of Jesus Christ to come out of her." And he came out that very hour (Acts 16:16-18).

That God would place that account so prominently in the book of Acts would seem sufficient to alert all who profess the Name of Christ against fortunetelling and any kind of divination. Notwithstanding the warning, never before in history has there been such a widespread interest in the psychic phenomena and the occult religions. There is nothing new about these practices.

When Paul the apostle was in Philippi, there was a girl who had the spirit of divination. We are not told in detail her various psychic powers, but undoubtedly, they included the telling of fortunes, locating of lost articles and informing people of secret matters. And thereby she could earn a handsome living for her masters. The divining spirit apparently was extremely subtle, more so than those which are openly antagonistic to the Gospel.

In this case, the spirit pretended to be a friend of Christ. From day to day, it annoyed Paul with its cry saying, "These men are the servants of the Most High God, who proclaim to us the way of salvation" (Acts 16:17). The spirit had a reason for what it was doing. If it would cause people to confuse Paul's preaching with the art of soothsaying, it would blunt the apostle's message. His ministry would be considered just another form of soothsaying.

This plan of mixing truth with error has been so successful that Satan has continued to use it to this day. For example, Jeane Dixon, who she says received her gift from a gypsy, claims the gift is the one mentioned in I Corinthians 12. We are also informed that by means of a crystal ball she is enabled to tell fortunes, predict the outcome of horse races, divine the winning number of a car raffle, etc. For years, she prepared horoscopes with the aid of astrology charts and is involved in various forms of psychic divination, all of which are condemned by the Scriptures (Isa. 47:13,14). At the same time, she considers herself a believer in Christ, as did the girl with the spirit of divination in Paul's day.

But the Apostle Paul was not deceived and eventually found it necessary to cast out the evil spirit. The girl, after being exorcised of the divining spirit, was no longer able to practice her soothsaying, much to her masters' indignation.

One of the most publicized of the psychics was the late Edgar Cayce. He came from a family that practiced divination. John Millard, in the book, *Edgar Cayce, Mystery Man of Miracles*, tells of Edgar's grandfather causing a heavy table to rise in the air and a broom to dance around the room without human aid.

There are serious consequences to playing with spirits. Once one allows these spirits to gain entrance into his home, he leaves a legacy of evil to his children and grandchildren. Edgar Cayce came from a family in which sorcery had become a game. Where the atmosphere is permissive to such things, these evil spirits will readily attach themselves to children, especially those whose nature may be particularly open to them. For Edgar, who was already a psychic, an accident seemed to have allowed the demons to secure an even more powerful hold upon him. A baseball struck the youth on the spine. Previously he had been quiet and reserved. Now his personality went through a striking transformation. He began to realize that he had a split personality.

The forces of good and evil were striving for supremacy. Young Cayce attended the Sam Jones Tabernacle in Hopkinsville, Kentucky. There he heard the powerful preaching of such men as D.L. Moody and George B. Pentecost. The young man had a long talk with Moody, who counseled with him to give himself to God. It could have been the turning point in his life, but somehow he could not seem to yield. It was the hour of decision, and Edgar failed to take advantage.

The spirits, which in time secured strong control of him, led Cayce into a troubled life. He half felt that his psychic powers were a gift from God, but at the same time, he was tormented with a suspicion that this power came from the devil. Mr. Millard records his saying, "How do I know this came from God? I've prayed for an answer to that, and there is none. There are evil forces, too. This could be the devil's power in disguise using me as an innocent tool to destroy others." How right he was!

Edgar Cayce in his youth had a sensitive conscience. Alas that he did not heed it fully. When he defied the devil and refused to operate his psychic powers, he seemed to be under a mysterious oppression from which he could not free himself. Mr. Millard says, "There was no longer any use in trying to pretend he was a normal human being with a will and freedom of choice. He was a puppet controlled by forces beyond human comprehension." And so he gave up resisting and continued his psychic readings.

But the devil is a poor paymaster. Besides the torment Cayce went through in the operation of his strange powers, death struck his home, and his small infant died. The mother, listless and withdrawn, sat staring into space. She contracted pneumonia and almost died. Fire destroyed his studio, plummeting him into a state of bankruptcy. His son, Hugh Lynn, was also killed in an explosion. His "gift" helped him not at all in planning his life. But the worst was yet to come.

While in a deep trance, the spirits led him into one of the worst delusions — reincarnation. At first he could not accept it. Then going into another trance, the spirits told him that man was ruled by the planets. Thus the spirit that dominated and ruled his life endorsed doctrines that were absolutely unscriptural (Isa. 47:13,14). These new "revelations" plunged Edgar Cayce deeper and deeper into the occult, including all the heathenish beliefs of transmigration of souls. His last days were marked by a series of misfortunes. At last, on January 3, 1945, his troubled soul went into eternity.

Such is the sad story of a man who was ruled by the spirits of sorcery and was led into the deepest of delusions. His life can only serve as an object lesson to warn others of the consequences of dabbling with the occult powers. These deceptive spirits have only one object in view, and that is to lead the gullible into confusion and finally to ruin their souls.

Despite the warnings which come from those who have wandered into these forbidden paths and have suffered the consequences, today tens of thousands of people continue to play with these spirits of divination and are thereby sowing seeds which will later result in a harvest of sorrow and woe.

Fortunetelling

There are a vast number of variations in the art of fortunetelling, from the psychic readings of Cayce to the fly-by-night operators who operate in the front room of a house which bears such a sign as: "Consult Madam X. She sees all, knows all, tells all." The madam usually has a crystal ball, burns incense, has an exotically decorated room where she meets with her clientele and tells their fortunes.

Some fortunetellers manipulate playing cards by which they presume to tell a person's future. To the lonely hearts: "You will meet a man — tall, dark and handsome." To the ambitious: "An unexpected fortune awaits you someday." To the suspicious: "Beware of the mysterious stranger." People visiting these fortunetellers often develop a strange compulsion to fulfill their predictions, clearly evidencing demonic influence.

Some prognosticators tell fortunes by examining and interpreting a person's palm. Others peer into the future through visions they profess to see. Still others claim they have the power to interpret dreams.

The present trend that seems to have caught the public's greatest fancy is fortunetelling by means of astrology. A person's future is said to be strongly influenced by the particular configuration of the heavens in the zodiac at the time of the individual's birth. By using charts which indicate the relative positions of the planets and the sun and moon, they pretend to tell their visitors which days are lucky, when to avoid or to enter into new business ventures, etc.

Astrology has had a long history. It was an art largely practiced by the ancients, who divided the zodiac into 12 parts. A personalized horoscope is prepared by reading and interpreting the relation of the planets to the fixed stars at the moment of a person's birth.

Proof of the fraudulent character of the whole astrological system is evident in the fact that three of the planets were unknown until the comparative recent invention of the telescope. When Uranus was discovered by Herschel in the 18th century, the astrology charts had to be substantially revised and arbitrary values attributed to the movement of that planet.

In the 19th century, Neptune was discovered, and the work of revision had to be repeated. Then in 1930, Pluto, the outermost planet, was spotted by Clyde Tombaugh at the Flagstaff Observatory, and again the charts had to be altered to conform to the new discovery.

Astrology is largely a pseudoscience of superstition. Nevertheless, as an occult art, it is associated with demonic powers. Merril F. Unger, in his excellent work *Demons in the World Today*, tells of a young man studying for the ministry who went to an astrologer and had a horoscope plotted. He thought to prove thereby that the system was fraudulent. But to his surprise and dismay, he discovered that its prophecies were coming true! This made the minister very uneasy. But he finally concluded that he had sinned in consulting the astrologer, acting in disobedience to the Word of God, and, therefore, had become the victim of occult powers. He repented of his act, and then found that the predictions were no longer correct. This was clear evidence that those who consult astrologers or fortunetellers of any kind place themselves under the influence of demonic powers.

Psychometry

Psychometry is a form of divination in which the operator touches clothing or some article belonging to the person from which information is desired. The individual possessing this "gift" is assumed able to secure impressions from the individuals who previously wore or possessed the article.

There are a number of professional psychometrists who claim to have these powers and their demonstrations on occasion are impressive. Among such individuals was Dunniger, the magician, who had remarkable success in locating hidden articles. In making his demonstration over a radio network, a committee would take an article and hide it some place in the city. Within a few minutes, Dunniger would be able to locate it. The magician denied possessing any supernatural powers, but attributed it to natural psychic ability. A most famous psychometrist was Peter Hurkos. On occasion, he identified murderers after being allowed to handle the weapon used in the crime.

The correct explanation of this phenomenon is of course found in the work of familiar spirits. It is merely another variety of fortunetelling.

When individuals who have had this form of divination hear the gospel message and express a desire to accept Christ, they immediately find a fierce opposition by the powers that had enabled them to perform their clairvoyant feats. Psychometry is clearly demonic in character.

Automatic Writing

Automatic writing is one of the most common methods used by occult artists. It is writing that is supposed to be produced by the spirits of the dead. Much of this is plain deception. Trick slates are used, which with a little clever jugglery, are shown to contain elaborate writing upon them. Some artists are so adept in this kind of deception that it is difficult for the amateur to detect the fraud.

However, there is some genuine automatic writing done by

spirits. Some mediums, when perfectly relaxed, find their fingers will write intelligible messages without conscious guidance. These usually purport to be from a dead friend or loved one of their client, though occasionally a message will be received from some historical character such as Caesar, Napoleon or Abraham Lincoln. This is only genuine in that it genuinely proceeds from the demonic realm.

The name of Ruth Montgomery came to the fore after she wrote the best-seller, *A Gift of Prophecy: The Phenomenal Jeane Dixon*, whom she declared to be a prophetess. Among the predictions she averred Mrs. Dixon made was a special revelation given her by a serpent who predicted that in the 1980s, a great man would arise who would start a new religion and bring in peace on earth. She made no mention about Christ, the Prince of Peace.

Later, Mrs. Montgomery, who made the rounds of the fortune-tellers, psychics, mediums and spiritist séances, suddenly discovered that she had become psychic herself. Although she acknowledges that she had been brought up a Methodist, she deserted her church in favor of psychic phenomena, which she came to believe had the answers to the great questions of life: "Why were we born? What is birth? Did we live before? Do personality and memory survive our passage through the door that man calls death?" She does not seek the answer to these questions from the Scriptures, but from the "spirits of the dead" with whom she believes she has established communication.

Mrs. Montgomery took a particular interest in automatic writing. Not having much success in her initial experiments, she consulted a friend advanced in the art, who gave her special instructions. She also bought a number of books on the subject and studied them carefully. To her great delight, when she tried automatic writing again, she found her pen came to life. It began to make all kinds of circles and curlicues. So powerful was the force that moved her hand that she said, "I could scarcely have stopped the nonsensical motions if I had tried." Her friend explained that the spirits were expressing their joy in being able to establish communication. Unfortunately for Mrs. Montgomery, the joy was the joy of demons. The lady little realized that she had turned her body over to the gyrations of foul spirits. One demon wrote exultingly, "I love you. Now you are mine." Indeed she was.

At this time, a "writing guide" took over. First it gave her much advice on buying and selling property. After this, the spirit got down to business. He told Mrs. Montgomery that automatic writing was one of the gifts spoken of by Paul in I Corinthians 12:7-11. She believed this and now sets aside a time each day to practice automatic writing. She was a little fearful at first that evil spirits were operating through her, so she prayed that no bad spirits would come. She little realized that bad spirits had already come.

Soon the spirits told her that they could get their messages through more easily if she put her fingers on a typewriter. When she did, she found her fingers dancing rapidly over the keys. When she read what was written, she found that "the messages" were more or less the philosophy of occultism. As for the resurrection of Christ with an actual body, this was strictly denied. Christ, the spirits said, could come and go as needed "without again having to wear the mantle of the earthly body. This was the message that was brought to the earth long ago by Christ."

This deceptive mixture of truth and error is clearly exposed and condemned by the Scriptures. John the apostle wrote, "Every spirit that does not confess that Jesus Christ has come in the flesh is not of God. And this is the *spirit* of the Antichrist" (I Jn. 4:3). Jesus came into the world clothed in flesh. When He was raised from the dead, He received a glorified body of flesh (Lk. 24:39). When He comes again, He will have the same body as He had when He went away (Acts 1:11).

The spirits, now having convinced Mrs. Montgomery to believe whatever was told her as truth, trotted out the old occult teaching of reincarnation that people are born, live, die, float around in space awhile, then are reincarnated through successive cycles of life, the same teaching that has cursed the countries of the East. These incredible delusions, including the belief that one's ancestors are reincarnated in cows and other animals, is truly the delusion of demons. They told her also that there was no death, the same lie that was told to Adam and Eve. They also informed her that the other planets of the solar system were inhabited. The spirits, true to type, denied that there was a devil. And that is Mrs. Montgomery's firm belief as she puts her fingers on the typewriter and more messages on reincarnation and occult philosophy are turned out at bewildering speed.

The Divining Rod

Many people are familiar with the divining rod or hazel twig. This kind of divination while not practiced extensively has its practitioners, especially in rural areas. The writer has met individuals from time to time who have witnessed such demonstrations. The diviner, or dowser, as he is sometimes called, is hired by owners of a certain tract of land to find water. As is well known, there are underground streams of water that run in certain strata levels that correspond to streams on the surface, not necessarily paralleling them, but running in independent directions. The problem is, of course, to find such a stream, for if a well is sunk over it, it will be fed by an abundant supply of water. Otherwise, it may be a dry hole.

The diviner claims that as he proceeds over the land with his divining rod or hazel branch, when he is over the vein of water, the twig will be drawn downward with a strong force. The evidence from many testimonies indicates that such demonstrations are often successful.

The question is, what is the force that affects the divining rod? There is not slightest doubt that the dowser is guided by clairvoyant powers. In most cases, the individual has little or no knowledge of the source of this force that moves his rod. It is clearly supernormal and must be classified with other similar practices as psychic in nature.

Hypnotic Demons

Every person has two minds — the conscious and the subconscious. When he is awake, the conscious mind is in control. When asleep, the subjective or subconscious mind operates. There is a fundamental difference between the two minds. The conscious mind has the power of discrimination and rejects anything that is obviously untrue. On the other hand, the subconscious mind believes every suggestion given it. If told there is a white elephant in the room, it fully believes it to be so.

In the case of hypnotism, the subject voluntarily surrenders his will to the hypnotist who leads him into a trance-like state in which the subconscious mind becomes the active one. The defenseless subconscious is ready to accept as fact whatever the hypnotist chooses to tell it. It is often claimed that a hypnotist cannot hypnotize a person against his will. Whether this is true or not remains to be proven; certainly, once an individual surrenders his will, he is at the whim of the hypnotist.

Now when a person yields his mind to that of another person, he has placed himself in a dangerous position. For it is in the psychic realm that evil and malicious spirits operate, waiting for a chance to enter and take control of a person's mind. The danger is not only during the period when the person is under the spell of hypnosis, but he is also subject to posthypnotic effects. The person at a certain moment will find himself doing something for which he can give no account or reason.

Morey Bernstein, in his book, *The Search For Bridey Murphey*, describes the tremendous power that the hypnotist has over the subject. The girl who was the subject of his experiments was supposedly regressed back before birth. Then she began to tell about a previous existence in Ireland as Bridey Murphey. In other words, it was a story of supposed reincarnation. Nevertheless, when the details were closely checked by *Life* magazine, it was found that many of the statements were false. The seducing spirits may have possessed an Irish person previously and could simulate the Irish vernacular; but many of the statements were so clearly false that they could only have come from lying spirits.

The extent to which hypnotism is being practiced by psychiatrists and kindred professions is alarming in view of the aftereffects. Certainly there is a direct link between this occult practice and demon activity.

To illustrate the dangers of hypnotism, let us take the documented case of Palle Hardrupp reported by Frank Edwards in *Stranger Than Science*. It is said that no one in a hypnotic trance will do anything contrary to his moral principles. But Hardrupp, under the influence of posthypnotic suggestion, was impelled to go into a bank in Copenhagen, Denmark, and shoot two officers in the bank. When Hardrupp came to trial for double murder, he had a strange story to tell. He had submitted to hypnosis, and the hypnotist, Bjorn Nielsen, had told him that he must rob the bank and shoot if the cashier resisted. Under the effects of the hypnotic spell, he was little more than a zombie. Having lost control of his will, he was compelled to commit a crime he could not avoid.

The trial was a sensation. Palle Hardrupp was found guilty of the murders and sentenced to a psychopathic ward. But that was not all. Nielsen was also indicted for inciting Palle into a state of hypnotic compulsion to commit the crime. Under psychiatric examination, Nielsen admitted he had conceived the plot to test his hypnotic powers. He was sentenced to life imprisonment for the crime of committing murder by hypnotism. One would be blind indeed not to see that demonic powers were involved in such practices.

One of the most knowledgeable men in the study of hypnosis, Dr. L.T. Woodward, says:

> I feel that hypnotism is too powerful a force to be used casually and for light entertainment. The science of understanding the mind is still in its infancy. Even the most expert of us feels a certain awe when he sees the incredible powers of hypnotism. Amateur hypnosis is to be strongly discouraged.

For Christians it is to be discouraged altogether. Hypnotism functions in the realm of the psychic, that is, a realm in which demons that are always lurking about may find entrance into the person. Then the subject's troubles begin. Just a few weeks before writing, a woman who once toyed with hypnotism came to the author with a sad story. For 17 years, these spirits had inhabited her mind and had almost driven her crazy with their chattering. Such spirits can be cast out, but the person often has a long battle with their attempts to return again.

UFOs

What is the nature and source of the UFO (Unidentified Flying Objects) phenomenon which has puzzled so many? There have been vast numbers of unexplained sightings. But never have any physical evidences of the flying saucers been found. The reason is simple. UFOs are not a physical but a spirit phenomenon.

Now the Word of God has given us a method of discerning between powers which are of God and evil powers. The apostle John gives us this: "Every spirit that does not confess that Jesus Christ has come in the flesh is not of God" (I Jn. 4:3). Those who claim to have made "contacts" with UFOs say that space visitors are soon to make further contacts with the human race in an attempt to save it from disaster. The alleged space visitors declare that they are of God, but they say nothing about the deity or Lordship of Jesus Christ. They pretend to come from other planets. Our own astronauts tell us that there is no evidence that physical beings could live on these planets — and these space visitors claim to be the same as human beings, only at a higher state of evolution!

After millions of reports of UFO sightings in recent years, even theologians are beginning to "admit" life beyond earth. One Jesuit priest and acclaimed astronomer in Argentina, Fr. Reyna, says it is time for man to relinquish his egocentric attitude and realize that God's creation of intelligent beings extends beyond earth.

Dr. Edward A. Boudreaux, associate professor of chemistry and a member of the American Chemical Society, the Chemical Society of London, the Louisiana Academy of Sciences and the Creation Research Society, has studied the UFO phenomenon exclusively, including cases of human encounters and communication with UFO occupants. He reports:

From these encounters, there emerges one unified pattern to the messages related to human contactees by UFO occupants:

1. They claim to be angels sent to prepare the way for the coming of Christ.

2. They warn mankind of great disasters to come, yet promise peace if we listen and obey their message.

3. They refer to the Creator but surprisingly do not call him God.

4. We are instructed to prepare ourselves spiritually by looking carefully within ourselves for higher spiritual qualities, and we should help others seek this same inner peace and joy of self.

5. They claim to come in peace (yet association with them has resulted in mysterious deaths, suicides, nervous breakdowns, sexual assaults, permanent psychological disturbances, public ridicule and many other adverse effects).

6. We are informed that the Kingdom of God is built by light and truth through meditation, and that we must think in this manner to attract space people who are creatures of light and not of darkness. This is the universal law of the Creator, they say, that we are spirit although we have physical bodies. We must learn to know our spiritual selves so as to communicate with the creatures of light who will show us the way to the kingdom of God.

These messages certainly are not what we would expect to hear from those who are preparing the way of the Lord; on the contrary, they have decided overtones of deceit as perpetuated by Satan. Thus it appears that UFO occupants are not messengers from God as claimed, but rather are messengers of Satan.

It is most disturbing that as popularity and interest in ufology continues to grow, even theologians and ministers are being deceived into thinking that UFOs may be messengers from God. Satan would like nothing better. *(Reprinted by permission from "Christian Life" magazine. Copyright August 1976, Christian Life Inc., Gundersen Dr. and Schmale Rd., Wheaton, IL 60187.)*

The Bible says nothing about a race of supermen coming from another planet to save the world from catastrophe! But it does have much to say about Christ's coming in the clouds of glory to judge the world (Matt. 25:31-46).

These so-called spacemen make no mention of the Bible way of salvation. Their favorite rendezvous is in the desert, where they reveal their "secrets" of saving the world from nuclear destruction. Christ had this to say about such desert visitors:

For false christs and false prophets will rise and show great signs and wonders to deceive, if possible, even the elect. See, I have told you beforehand. Therefore if they say to you, "Look, He is in the desert!" do not go out; *or* "Look, *He is* in the inner rooms!" do not believe *it* (Matt. 24:24-26).

The whole UFO story does not ring true. It has the earmarks of the diabolical. It is in fact nothing but sorcery, a psychic manifestation, and the work of demons. It is indeed a delusion of evil spirits that has bewitched many people. Let no Christian fall for it.

Chapter Seventeen

Witchcraft: Black and White Magic

The book of Acts gives a number of instances in which certain individuals were engaged in magic, commonly spoken of as "black magic" or "white magic." This of course is plain sorcery, involving the operation of demons. Its first mention in the Acts is of one Simon the Sorcerer:

> But there was a certain man called Simon, who previously practiced sorcery in the city and astonished the people of Samaria, claiming that he was someone great (Acts 8:9).

Simon bewitched the people with his sorceries, no doubt demonstrating certain preternatural phenomena, such as charms, spells, incantations. However, when confronted with the powerful ministry of Philip, James and John, he had to confess that here was a greater power. Simon had engaged in his nefarious traffic so long that there was no moral conviction on his part. To him, this kind of magic was "Jesus magic," a kind stronger than others. He saw that the power of the apostles was greater than any he had known. He witnessed their casting out many demons and spirits of divination. Simon was determined to get the same power, and assumed it could be bought with money. Peter quickly exposed the evil nature of Simon's thoughts and rebuked him severely:

Peter said to him, "Your money perish with you, because you thought that the gift of God could be purchased with money! You have neither part nor portion in this matter, for your heart is not right in the sight of God. Repent therefore of this your wickedness, and pray God if perhaps the thought of your heart may be forgiven you" (Acts 8:20-22).

Simon, struck with terror by Peter's denunciation, asked him to pray that none of these things should come upon him. There is no evidence that there was any real change of heart on Simon's part, and tradition tells us that he was a leading influence in founding the false cult of gnosticism.

Another instance mentioned in Acts is the case of Bar-Jesus of Paphos (Acts 13:6-12). He also is called a sorcerer, and he withstood Paul, who was persuading Sergius Paulus, the deputy, to accept the faith. Paul rebuked the man, calling him "son of the devil," thus revealing his connection with the demonic powers (Acts 13:10). At the same instant, a judgment of blindness came upon the man. Thus a precedent was set, justifying direct action against those who attempt to ply the black arts against preachers of the Gospel. The scathing denunciation that the Apostle Paul gave him indicates God's condemnation of all those who practice these arts.

The book of Exodus speaks of the magicians of Pharaoh who also had certain powers and could simulate some of the miracles of Moses and Aaron. Paul refers to them by name as Jannes and Jambres, the men who withstood Moses and likened them to those who practiced the black arts. He warned that as time went on, men would get worse and worse. "But evil men and impostors will grow worse and worse, deceiving and being deceived" (II Tim. 3:13).

The practices of these men find their fulfillment today in the various sorceries of our day. Generally, those engaged in these operations deny any involvement with demonic spirits, but regard their art as involving purely psychological phenomena. Strange as it may seem, in recent years, a new breed of witches and wizards are appearing on the scene who openly confess that they are in league with the devil! With incredible audacity, they boast of their power as coming from Satan, and strangely enough, they are finding followers. Even as the Scriptures teach against the works of the flesh, these exponents of satanism glorify and praise every kind of deviation and abomination.

Devil Worship

> Then the devil, taking Him up on a high mountain, showed Him all the kingdoms of the world in a moment of time. And the devil said to Him, "All this authority I will give You, and their glory; for *this* has been delivered to me, and I give it to whomever I wish. Therefore, if You will worship before me, all will be Yours" (Lk. 4:5-7).

Satan offered Jesus the kingdoms of the world if He would but fall down and worship him. Of course, Satan ignominiously failed. Nevertheless, the devil and his army of demons continue even yet in their attempts to promote satanic worship.

Among primitive people, devil worship is a common thing. Paul in his letter to the Corinthians speaks of such worship among the gentiles:

> Rather, that the things which the Gentiles sacrifice they sacrifice to demons and not to God, and I do not want you to have fellowship with demons. You cannot drink the cup of the Lord and the cup of demons; you cannot partake of the Lord's table and of the table of demons (I Cor. 10:20,21).

That the heathen worship the devil is well known, but that this diabolical practice has found acceptance in America, is indeed astonishing, and that it should find so many followers is incredible. *The National Observer*, October 13, 1969, has this to say about the rise of satanism:

> For obvious reasons Satanism is the most obscure mani-

festation of witchcraft. Yet one audacious operator has promoted it into a full-time religion, complete with liturgy, weekly services, and tax exemption. In 1966, Anton Szander LaVey founded the First Satanic Church in San Francisco dedicated to indulgence, sex, vengeance, and all sins.

Inside the black-painted house on California Street, a visitor is shown to a fully lighted living room with solid black walls and a hell-fire red ceiling. A stuffed owl peers from atop a black coffin that stands on end beside a stone fireplace. The mantle of the fireplace, the visitor is informed, holds "the vital living altar" — a voluptuous nude priestess who reclines there during the church services.

The 30-year-old high priest, with shaved skull, mustache drooping into pointed goatee, bears a striking resemblance to the popular image of Lucifer himself.

Newsweek (August 16, 1971) says concerning the rise of satanism in America:

Today tens of thousands across the U.S. — some of them middle-class adults with advanced degrees — are dabbling in Satanism, witchcraft, voodoo, and other forms of black or white magic. Some of it is pure fantasy, but a good deal of the arcane experimentation results from plain blind faith in Satan's power which sometimes produces macabre acts of violence and sex, that in less enlightened eras of U.S. history would have brought the perpetrators swift punishment at the stake.

The magazine describes a killing by a long-hair satanist girl convicted of manslaughter for stabbing a 62-year-old man to death. "I really enjoyed killing him," she said.

Anton Szander LaVey now claims 10,000 dues-paying members. *Newsweek* adds, "White magic is spreading as fast as witches can organize covens. There are some 80,000 'white witches' in the United States, estimates father Richard Woods." The amazing growth of witchery and the worship of Satan indicates that this form of demon activity has tremendously increased in the last few years, preparing the way for the universal worship of the dragon, or the devil, during the Great Tribulation (Rev. 13:4).

Witchcraft in England

It is estimated that there are tens of thousands of witches in the British Isles. Certainly there are enough people in London interested in witchcraft to justify the large number of stores specializing in African and Eastern sorcery. Walking through the Charing Cross area, one will be overwhelmed with the number of books on witchcraft, amulets, talismans and encyclopedias on demonology and occultism. Countless covens meet frequently throughout London. Not a few occurrences get into the newspaper — such as an ad some years ago by the Duke of Leinster seeking a witch with powers to break a "curse" that was placed on his family years ago.

One case involved the John Durstons, who claimed that a rambunctious ghost was creating havoc in their apartment. Furniture was moved from one place to the other. The radio went on and off. Misty fingers could be seen from time to time swirling around the place. The village vicar, Rev. Gordon Langford, was called in, and as a result of his investigation, reported the circumstances to his superior, Bishop Robert Mortimor. The bishop decided to exorcise the spirit. Apparently he was successful, except the spirit moved to another apartment and carried on its mischievous operations there.

Chapter Eighteen

Witchcraft in Foreign Lands

Idol Worship

> What am I saying then? That an idol is anything, or what is offered to idols is anything? Rather, that the things which the Gentiles sacrifice they sacrifice to demons and not to God, and I do not want you to have fellowship with demons (I Cor. 10:19,20).

The words of Paul very clearly associate idol worship with demon worship. It is commonly supposed that an idol is merely a chunk of wood or metal shaped by a craftsman. But when such an image is dedicated to some deity and is worshiped, a strange affinity seems to develop between the idol and a demon. Certain preternatural manifestations often appear in connection with idol worship; that is why idolatry has gotten such a stronghold upon the heathen. The idol is an object of worship and a center for demons to cluster around. That is why the prophets ordered the destruction of idols. They burned them and ground them to powder, not only to keep people from worshiping them, but to destroy the evil liaison between the idol and the demon. Because of this strange affinity, Paul warned Christians not to partake in any of the idolatrous ceremonies or rituals, nor even to eat in an idol temple.

This relation between idol worship and demons is revealed in the song of Moses. The patriarch foresaw that Israel would abandon their Creator and make light of the Rock of their salvation" (Deut. 32:15). That led to idolatry, and the worship of demons:

> They sacrificed to demons, not to God, to *gods* they did not know, to new *gods*, new arrivals that your fathers did not fear (Deut. 32:17).

The Demons of Juju

In Nigeria, demon forces work under the magic of juju. The forces of evil are very great, and those who are not under the blood are subject to their power. While in Nigeria, my daughter Carole thought stories being told us about juju were exaggerated. Rev. S.G. Elton informed her that under certain circumstances in that country where there is so much witchcraft and worship of the devil, very mysterious and evil things can happen. She was not fully convinced.

Going to her room that very day, however, she had a most enlightening experience. A powerful demon entered the room, and as she looked up, she could feel a powerful, hostile force in the room. It began to press against her. She began to rebuke it, but taken by surprise, she was not successful in ejecting the evil power. She rushed out of her room, came to Brother Elton and me, and told us of her combat with unseen powers. By steadily rebuking it in the Name of Jesus, she had been able to keep it from taking possession of her, but she had not been successful in driving it away.

Brother Elton and I then went to the room and rebuked the juju demon in the Name of Jesus. Our sharp rebuke drove it away, and it attacked Carole no more. She was by now well convinced of the reality of these powerful demons that roam the dark places in Africa.

While many incidents could be told of the operations of juju, space requires us to restrict ourselves to one incident told by a young man by the name of Ekpo Uma and fully confirmed by Brother Elton.

Ekpo attended a meeting in Nigeria and became convinced of the truth of the Gospel. He was converted to Christ and became a member of a local church. He even began to do some preaching.

About this time, a juju man came to visit him. The man said, "You sing a song, 'There is no power to hinder the work of the Lord,' but I tell you there is a power that will hinder the work of the Lord."

"Not so," said Ekpo. "I know there are other powers, but none so great as the power of the Lord."

Then Ekpo made a mistake. Not being very knowledgeable on the matter of the working of the juju demons, he let the juju worker sleep in his house that night. In the morning he left, after saying that he would see that there was a higher power — the power of juju, and added that he would send thunder on the house to kill him.

That night in the room where he slept there shone a supernatural light. He awakened his wife to pray with him. Ekpo tells what happened next:

> When I knelt to pray, there appeared to be another being under my bed, and it took hold of me. The strange being picked me up and threw me out of the window. My whole body was lighted up with a flame. I cried out to God and began to rebuke the thing. While these strange flames were about me, I ran to the police station. As I started to answer, I was overwhelmed by that evil spirit. The police beat me and threw me into a cell.
>
> Meanwhile the people in the church heard what had happened, and they began to pray for my deliverance. One night I saw the angel of the Lord coming into my cell. He reached down and touched the strong iron chain and broke it. Then the angel left.
>
> A strange thing happened then. My spirit left my body. I could hear the people around me saying, "He is dead. He is dead." In the morning the people came to get my dead corpse, but then I opened my eyes. The doctor said no treatment was necessary; the trouble was mental. But

the people of the church kept on praying. Time went by, and they took me to the church where Christians began to pray for me. God's power came down, and the Lord completely healed me.

Pastor Elton then took me into his Bible school training course. Since my experience with the dreaded juju, I have prayed for others and seen them delivered from its evil power. At the present time I am translating books, including those used in the Christ For The Nations crusade into the Efik language.

Voodoo

Voodoo was originally imported from Africa. Its practice is most common in the countries of the Caribbean, especially Haiti, Dominican Republic and Jamaica. This form of sorcery has captured the popular imagination more than any other, and many are the stories of its frenzied rites. It is demon worship in one of its most intense forms.

The voodoo ritual is usually held in the open, under a moonlit sky. These rites are generally carried out far from the city in a secluded, tree-encircled section of a plantation, or they may be held in a cave or an abandoned barn.

The prominent feature of the ritual is the rhythmic drumbeat. The participants stand in a circle around a central fire. A vessel stands nearby which contains a large quantity of rum. Between the drumbeats can be heard the voice of people who are squatting or standing about the fire. One man leads the chanting as the drumbeat becomes louder and faster, weaving a hypnotic spell over the people. Bodies weave and sway to the rhythm of the drums.

Alcohol, drugs and the incessant chanting all combine to provide a mass hysteria. In this atmosphere, demons find favorable conditions to drive their devotees to the wildest excesses. The whole scene degenerates into an orgiastic riot. As C.H. Wallace says in his *Witchcraft in the World Today*, "They do as they feel possessed by spirits evoked by the chanting. ... But even without direct hypnotism, the ritual itself will induce the feeling of sudden possession — of being controlled by something other than one's own free will." This something of course is the voodoo demons.

The voodoo rites gradually come to an end as men and women writhe on the ground under the influence of the drugs and the satanic spirits that possess them.

Closely associated with voodooism are the zombies, or the "walking dead." Many consider these creatures mythical. The natives believe that zombies are without living instincts, but function like robots, coming out of the grave at nightfall and returning again at dawn.

The Firewalkers

In some parts of Africa there are firewalkers. Rev. J.L. de Bruin showed us an amazing documentary film of their practices involving the walking on coals of fire at a temperature over 800 degrees centigrade. He had visited a Hindu tribe who lived in South Africa and watched their ceremonies.

In preparation for their act, firewalkers fast 14 days for "purification," explaining that to walk on fire, they must be possessed with spirits — evil spirits — and the purification necessary. When they complete their fast, they will make preparation for their ceremonies, using as much as 14 tons of wood to make a firebed on which they worship the fire goddess.

While the firebed is being prepared, they will make sacrifice of animals to the goddess of blood. With a blunt instrument called a machete, they make one stroke and cut off a goat's head. Then a woman under the influence of the spirit standing nearby will grab the goat and drink the blood while the heart pumps. The devotees in their rite of purification, go to the nearest river to wash. The priests then pray that the spirits will help them, and while the music plays, the spirits enter their bodies. Their breathing at this point takes on a strange pulsation. While being possessed of a spirit, their bodies become absolutely limp and numb so that up to 150 hooks can be placed into the flesh. Brass containers with various offerings, weighing as much as 150 pounds, may be hung on these hooks.

J.L. de Bruin Accepts a Challenge

Ordinarily a Christian does not accept the challenge of these heathen rites. As Jesus said to Satan, *"You shall not tempt the LORD your God"* (Matt. 4:7). But de Bruin wanted to help these people as he watched them walk on fire. Remembering the challenge of Elijah on Mt. Carmel, he decided that the only way he could help them was to show that Christ gave him power over fire without the help of these evil spirits. We will let him tell the story:

> While sitting at the firebed watching the unusual things that they were performing, my spirit was greatly disturbed. I said, "Lord, what can a Christian that is filled with the Holy Spirit of God do — if these people can do these unusual things while possessed of an evil spirit?" These people sedately walked through a bed of fire 33 feet long, ten feet wide, and ten inches deep with red-hot, burning coals.
>
> For no reason at all one of these heathen men turned around to me and said, "Sir, you see what we Hindus can do? And no Christian is able to do it in the whole world. We have never had a Christian that can walk through fire in bare feet as we do. It can never be done."
>
> This had an effect on me. That a Hindu man possessed of evil spirits could tell me that no Christian in the world is able to do what they do. I either had to defend my Christianity or be defeated, and I didn't feel that I could be defeated. I prayed in my heart how to answer this man. All of a sudden I felt a very great calmness come over me.
>
> I asked the man, "Now what would you do if a Christian would walk with his bare feet across this bed of fire?"

And he said, "Sir, we will not call it a miracle, but we will call it an outstanding miracle, for it will just have to be one. We had two white people before who tried to walk the firebed, but they were so badly burned that they were laid up for six weeks in the hospital." (Afterwards, I found out that they were two spiritualists.)

So I walked around the firebed. They said, "If you are going to walk the firebed, we cannot take responsibility for you."

I said, "No, you don't have to."

They said, "You must take your socks off, or your socks will catch fire." I took my socks off. It may seem strange to you that a Christian at a heathen ceremony would attempt to walk through a bed of red-hot, burning coals, 800 degrees Fahrenheit. But there is a Scripture in Isaiah 43:2 (KJV), where the Lord said: "When thou passest through the waters ... they shall not overflow thee." Moses had that experience at the Red Sea. Joshua had that experience at the River Jordan. The prophets Elijah and Elisha had the very same experience when they walked through the water — it did not overflow them. The Scripture goes on to say: "When thou walkest through the fire, thou shalt not be burned; neither shall the flame kindle upon thee." That is a very strong Scripture for any Christian to stand upon. And the Word of God can never change, though heaven and earth pass away.

I looked up to heaven and said, "Father, in the name of Jesus, I ask for Your protection." Then I entered that firebed with my bare feet, and I came out the other side.

These heathen people shouted to me, "You will never do that again!" I went back for a second time. They cried out to me, "You will never do it a third time." And I went back to that firebed for the third time, with my bare feet. They surrounded me and searched my feet and were amazed that there was not a burn or a blister on my feet where the fire had touched me. God had protected me, and I was able to uphold the power of the Word of God and the power of the Spirit of God. Jesus Christ is the same yesterday, today, and forever.

It also gave me an opportunity to preach to the people and to tell them that they may be able to walk through firebeds, and hook their bodies and skewer their tongues, but the gods whom they serve can never open blind eyes, and cause cancers to fall out, and make the cripples to walk, and cleanse and purge the sinner's conscience from dead works, that he may be able to serve the living God.

While I was walking through the firebeds, a man stood there with a camera and made a movie of my going through the firebeds. I bought this piece of film from him, and today I have in my possession documentary film that a Christian was able to walk through a red-hot, burning fire with his bare feet to prove that anything can be done in the name of the Lord, if we'll trust and believe.

And so it was again as in the days of Moses and Elijah. The magicians were able to turn their rods into serpents, but Moses' rod swallowed up theirs. Christ's power is always greater than Satan's.

Chapter Nineteen

The Demons of Spiritism

Spiritism has had a long history, but its modern revival began comparatively recently in 1844 under the Fox sisters. To any enlightened person, spiritism (commonly called spiritualism by those who make a religion of it) has no appeal. It is soundly condemned by the Scriptures. Indeed witches (today often called by a more respected name, mediums) under the Mosaic law were to be put to death.

To people unlearned in the Scriptures who have lost their loved ones through death, the prospect of being able to communicate with them has a certain appeal. But spiritism's teaching that the spirits of the dead float around haunting houses, living as ghosts tapping on walls is a poor substitute indeed compared to the sublime revelation of the Scriptures that the righteous are conveyed to the regions of paradise. The words of Jesus in Luke 16:19-31 definitely establish the fact that no communication is possible between the living and the spirits of the dead. Consequently those spirits with whom mediums pretend to communicate are not the spirits of deceased relatives but are evil spirits which impersonate them.

Although a great deal of trickery goes on in the séances, especially among mediums whose psychic powers have faded, the evidence is overwhelming that there is actual communication with the spirit world, but not with the spirits of loved ones who have departed this life.

The whole subject of spiritualism is encompassed in a web of deception and delusion. Although spiritualists often quote the Scriptures in their attempts to give their beliefs scriptural sanction and some respectability, they are careful to avoid all passages which expose spiritism as the work of impersonating spirits. The Scriptures are not regarded as the final authority by these people, but they arbitrarily choose a few passages out of context, conveniently ignoring those which openly condemn the trafficking in spirits and declare it to be the work of Satan.

The fact is that the Bible is very emphatic in its condemnation of all kinds of sorcery and witchcraft. Here are a few of the Scriptures:

> And the person who turns to mediums and familiar spirits, to prostitute himself with them, I will set My face against that person and cut him off from his people. ... A man or a woman who is a medium, or who has familiar spirits, shall surely be put to death; they shall stone them with stones. Their blood *shall be* upon them (Lev. 20:6,27).

> There shall not be found among you *anyone* who makes his son or his daughter pass through the fire, *or one* who practices witchcraft, *or* a soothsayer, or one who interprets omens, or a sorcerer, or one who conjures spells, or a medium, or a spiritist, or one who calls up the dead. For all who do these things *are* an abomination to the LORD, and because of these abominations the LORD your God drives them out from before you. ... For these nations which you will dispossess listened to soothsayers and diviners; but as for you, the LORD your God has not appointed such for you (Deut. 18:10-12,14).

Spiritism can best be described by its utter triviality. Compared with the sublime truths of the Scriptures, the babble of the spirits is often profane and irrelevant to any of the real issues of life. Lying and mendacity are the trademarks of its communications. As a whole, its teachings are a flat contradiction of the great redemptive truths revealed in the Bible.

The familiar spirits which operate through the medium enter into a sort of covenant relationship with the person who is in a real sense in league with the devil. While certain insane spirits reduce their victims to a state of imbecility, spiritist demons have an even more sinister objective: to deceive people. Consequently the seducing spirit or spirits that take over a medium allows its deluded host a certain amount of liberty. However, as the years go by, the presence of foul spirits often has a devastating effect upon the personality of their victim.

Some mediums lose their minds altogether and actually become psychotic. In the case of Peter Hurkos, the action of the spirits have so disrupted his life that he heartily wishes that he had never heard of his "psychic gift." The last years of the Fox sisters, who are considered the founders of modern spiritualism, were pitiful beyond description. The sisters had become confirmed alcoholics. When they finally saw that spiritism had ruined their lives, they renounced it publicly and with vehemence. The American press described Margaret as "an object of charity, a mental and physical wreck, whose appetite is only for intoxicating liquors. ... The lips that utter little else than profanity, once promulgated the doctrine of a new religion which still numbers its tens of thousands of enthusiastic believers."

Once a spiritualist medium opens up to the spirits, many of them will flock to her clamoring for an audience, creating a great confusion. Satan, who is king of both the fallen angels and demons, however, has instituted a certain kind of order in the spirit world. He knows that confusion of this nature will not promote his work. Shortly after a person becomes a medium, therefore, one of the more powerful spirits (usually representing itself as the spirit of a deceased human), will arrive on the scene, take command of the situation and represent himself as the "guide." From henceforth other demons may only communicate to the medium through the offices of the "guide."

The Case of the Witch of En Dor

The episode of Saul's visit to the witch of En Dor has afforded much controversy, but regarding the lesson that it teaches of divine disapproval of necromancy or the consulting of the dead, there can be no doubt.

Saul, because of his stubbornness and disobedience, eventually found that God answered him no more. He then determined to consult a witch, a woman with a familiar spirit, or in today's terminology, a medium. Saul requested of the woman to bring up Samuel. After some hesitation, she proceeded to go through her usual preparation which undoubtedly meant going into a trance. Until then, Saul had concealed his identity. But then suddenly something quite unexpected happened. The medium was overcome with terror and began to scream in fright. Of what actually happened, there is some difference of opinion. Ordinarily the impersonating spirit pretends to be the spirit of the departed dead. Many expositors believe that this was the case this time.

Others, however, believe that God intervened in this particular case and permitted the real Samuel to return. If so, this exception is a very unique case, for Jesus in speaking of Lazarus and the rich man declared that the dead do not communicate with the living (Lk. 16:19-31).

One thing is clear, the episode is recorded in detail in the Scriptures as a grim warning against seeking after those with familiar spirits to attempt to communicate with the dead. The colloquy between Samuel (if it were indeed Samuel) and Saul is highly significant. In the severest terms, Samuel rebuked the king, told him that the kingdom would be wrested from him, and that on the next day, both he and his sons would die.

As we have said, this account is a clear indication that all attempts to communicate with the dead are divinely forbidden. I Chronicles 10:13 declares that one of the reasons that judgment came upon Saul was that he had consulted a witch:

> Saul died for his unfaithfulness which he had committed

against the LORD, because he did not keep the word of the LORD, and also because he consulted a medium for guidance.

Spiritism and Haunted Houses

As everyone is aware, there are reports of houses in which there have been heard mysterious rappings, and sometimes fleeting apparitions have been seen. What is the explanation of these strange and ghostly phenomena? That these noises and disturbances are caused by evil spirits there can be no doubt.

What is the cause of these preternatural visitations? Investigation has shown that usually sometime in the past there was violence in the house, and this in some way was impinged into the atmosphere of the place. Professor Nandoor Fodor makes a philosophical statement which Bible students can perhaps accept. He says, "Nothing apparently which happens in the universe ever perishes, particularly nothing which happens to the human mind or soul." This reminds us of the words of Jesus in Matthew 12:36,37:

> But I say to you that for every idle word men may speak, they will give account of it in the day of judgment. For by your words you will be justified, and by your words you will be condemned.

There is, of course, one exception. God has promised to blot out our transgressions. They cease to exist as a fact in the universe (Isa. 43:25). We can thank God for that.

But to the subject of ghosts. There is no doubt that ghostly rappings are caused by evil spirits as shown in the case of the Fox sisters who succeeded in communicating with them, an event which initiated the fad of modern spiritualism. There is a definite relation between these ghostly manifestations and that of spiritualism. Since mediums traffic in these spirits, it is not strange that they have been called upon to exorcise spirits from haunted houses.

As Christ taught, evil spirits have a strong desire to enter a human body (Lk. 11:24-26). The body of a medium has been conditioned to receive these spirits. Hence when a medium goes to a house where a "ghost spirit" is, the latter immediately senses an affinity with the medium. There, the instant the medium goes into a trance, the "ghost spirit" rushes into his body.

William Oliver Stevens in his book *Unbidden Guests* tells of a case involving the medium Eileen Garrett and Dr. Nandoor Fodor. The services of a medium were retained to expel a ghost from a house of a dissolute couple.

The ghost made its appearance several nights by loud knocking. On the fourth night, the husband awoke to see an old man dressed in a tunic and leggings with a kerchief at the neck. The husband addressed the figure, and when the man did not answer, the husband became angry and rushed at him to throw him out. His hands passed through the old man's body. The husband ran to the wife's room and fainted. She saw the old man and demanded an explanation. Receiving no answer she struck at him, and her hands went through the apparition and struck the door.

The visitations continued for some time. On one occasion, the old man showed the couple that his throat has been cut from ear to ear. At this point, they solicited the aid of Dr. Fodor. The doctor in turn sought the help of the medium Eileen Garrett. Meeting in the bedroom of the house, Mrs. Garrett went into a trance and her spirit control, Urami, began to speak through her. The spirit replied that the unpleasant emotional tensions existing in the house between the couple produced a favorable atmosphere for the ghost to manifest itself. To rid the house of the ghost, it must be allowed to take possession of the medium. They could then communicate directly with the spirit.

The medium went into a trance, and the ghost entered her. She became rigid and started fumbling at her throat. The ghost claimed that it had been a landholder in the 16th century. His lord had seduced the landholder's wife and left him to die in a dungeon. (Such stories of course are fabrications.)

The ghost was made to understand that it was no longer to disturb the household. The control spirit of a medium has certain power over other spirits, and it gave orders to the "ghost" spirit, which shows there is an authority structure even in Satan's kingdom.

This is necessary, for if all the demons who desired took permanent quarters in mediums, they would be destroyed, and that of course would put an end to spiritualism, which is one of Satan's favorite means of deluding people.

But it must be added that persons who are not mediums and who purposely open themselves to demons will find that these spirits, once they get control of a person, are almost impossible to shake off. They remain to torment their victims and may succeed in driving them to insanity.

Much has been written in psychic circles about haunted houses, the tappings, the footsteps on stairs, the fleeting apparitions. Spiritualists claim that the spirits which produce these phenomena are those of the departed dead. Spiritists as a rule do not recognize nor concede that there are demon spirits. Few mediums are ready to advertise that they are operating under the influence of demons.

In May 1958, Rev. Maxwell Whyte was summoned to help exorcise spirits from a house in Oshawa, Ontario. The owner and occupier was Mrs. A. On. Upon arrival he found the lady distraught and unable to sleep without sedatives because of things that had been happening. Strange footsteps were heard on the hardwood floor of the hallway. Glasses would rattle violently in the middle of the night. A white cat and an elderly lady were seen in the bathroom, and then both suddenly disappeared.

What was the cause of these things? Rev. Whyte, writing in *The Voice of Healing* magazine, November 1958, said: "At least two of the families that lived previously in the house were godless people. One or more were demon possessed. On the death of one of these persons, the demons would roam around the house seeking another godless person in whom to dwell. A demon does not like to be cast out or deprived of a body at death. When a Christian woman (Mrs. On) and her family moved into this house, the demons were greatly disappointed because they could not enter into a bloodwashed child of God; therefore, their only recourse was to scare out the Christians and get in some other godless family and enter their bodies."

Pastor Whyte, having made this explanation, moved about through the house, pleading the blood of Jesus in every room and around the perimeter of the property. The haunting spirits were commanded to leave in the Name of Jesus. The demons were quite stubborn and hung around for three or four days, and then left altogether.

Pastor Whyte has had similar experiences since, and has been uniformly successful in exorcising these annoying spirits. It might be added that spirits cannot produce these phenomena in every house, but usually where these manifestations occur, there have lived persons in the place previously who were unusually wicked or who had committed some vicious crime.

Ghosts

Suzanna Wesley, writing to her oldest son Sam on January 12, 1716, told of certain ghostly rappings in their house:

> The reason of our fears is as follows. On the first of December our maid heard at the door of the dining room several dismal groans, like a person in extremes, at the point of death. We gave little heed to her fears. Some nights (two or three) after, several of the family heard a strange knocking in divers places, usually three or four knocks at a time, and stayed a little. This continued every night for a fortnight; sometimes it was in the garret, but mostly in the nursery, or green chamber.

This was the beginning of ghostly phenomena that plagued the Wesley household for two months. The affair is well documented because the details appear in the family's letters and John Wesley's journal. The town of Epworth where the Wesley rectory was located was inhabited by people "long known for their activities in witchcraft and the darker arts." The Wesleys had several misfortunes there during their stay. There were two fires in the rectory, one of which almost resulted in the death of young John. The rebuilding was expensive, and Samuel Wesley, the father, at one time was sent to a debtor's prison because he could not pay his debts.

In addition to the moaning and knocking and rapping, there were footsteps going up and down the stairs all night. These occurrences naturally caused the children to be frightened. The father was the last one to be informed of the affair. When told, he concluded the noises were the result of the pranks of some of the children. Nevertheless, the rappings continued. Mrs. Wesley thought the disturbances might be caused by rats and weasels. Steps were taken to drive away the supposed pests, but the rappings only became louder and more persistent.

Then it was Mr. Wesley's turn to hear the ghostly rappings. When in bed one night, he heard nine loud knocks on the wall by his bedside — that rapping being in groups of three. Still wondering if the noises were not being made by one of the children, he got up and searched the house and the grounds but could find nothing. He then bought a large watchdog, hoping the dog would discover the culprits. But the next day there were six rappings, and the dog after barking in a fury suddenly became silent and began to grovel in terror.

By now Mr. Wesley was thoroughly alarmed. The noises of people walking, of money being emptied out, and other sounds occurring during the night had him dismayed. The mother, in writing to her son, said, "All in the family heard it together, in the same room, at the same time, particularly at family prayers. It always seemed to all present in the same place at the same time, though often before any could say it was here, it would remove to another place."

As time went on, the knockings got worse. Mr. Wesley finally out of temper chased the turmoil around the house beating on joists and rafters, but to no avail. In his anger, he pulled a pistol and was about to shoot at the spot where the knocks were coming from. A neighbor who was present calmed him down and said, "Sir, you are convinced this is something supernatural. If so, you cannot hurt it."

This seemed to give Mr. Wesley a new thought and he cried out,

"Thou dumb and deaf devil, why dost thou frighten these children that cannot answer for themselves? Come to me to my study that am a man." There was one more knock, and that ended things for the night. Sure enough, the spirit left the rest of the house to appear in the study. There all sorts of strange phenomena took place — latches lifted of themselves, doors opened, and even a bed was levitated. Some of the family even saw a man walking down the stairs with a long white robe. Others saw what appeared to be a badger-like animal.

Apparently Mr. Wesley, observing that he had driven the spirit from the other part of the house to his study, came to realize that this was the way that the spirit could be cast out. Jesus said, "In My name they will cast out demons" (Mk. 16:17). While we do not have complete details, apparently the clergyman rebuked the ghostly spirit until it ceased its disturbances. At any rate, the noises stopped.

In analyzing the incident, two other points could be mentioned. The town was given over to witchcraft and sorcery. Evil spirits find it favorable to operate in an atmosphere of this kind. Second, John Wesley and his brother, Charles, were destined to be the instruments in the hands of God to bring a revival to England such as was never known before. The revival saved England from the otherwise atheistic chaos that afflicted France during the French Revolution. Demons are not all-wise; yet they do have foreknowledge of certain events. It is not unlikely that the evil spirits had some precognition that God was to use these young men in a way that would wreak serious damage to the kingdom of darkness. Hence it would be to their great advantage if the knocking could get the family sidetracked into an interest in the occult.

That is what happened in the Fox family. The two sisters Margaret and Kate got to playing with spirits and eventually became mediums and founders of modern spiritualism. John Wesley became the founder of Methodism. Evidently Wesley's father recognized the rappings for what they were — evil spirits seeking communication with humans. They were exorcised from the home, and John Wesley grew to manhood to become the apostle of the 18th century.

Reincarnation

Webster's Dictionary, unabridged edition, defines reincarnation as follows: "The belief involved in various doctrines of metempsychoses and transmigration of souls, that the souls of the dead successively return to the earth in new forms or bodies; hence a rebirth of a soul in a new, especially a human body."

Those who hold to the doctrine of reincarnation have many theories: (1) Reincarnation at death, without memory of any previous life; (2) Progressive reincarnation: gross people are reborn in subhuman (animal) bodies, refined people in progressive states of existence; (3) At death, people go to another plane of conscious existence, later to return voluntarily to the earth plane.

Necromancy or spiritualism, messages from the world of spirits, tends largely to endorse some variety of reincarnation. These are lying spirits, or demons, for they flatly deny the Scripture teaching summed up in Hebrews 9:27, "It is appointed for men to die once, but after this the judgment." Some reincarnationists grasp at the words of Jesus, "You must be born again" (Jn. 3:7) as confirming the doctrine. This conclusion is patently false, as shown by the context, for when Nicodemus tried to apply the statement in a physical sense, Jesus at once set him right and showed His words referred to spiritual birth.

From a purely philosophic view, apart from the Scriptures, Jay Hudson in his *Law of Psychic Phenomena* says:

> I do not know anything about reincarnation. I know as much about it, however, as anyone else knows. I mean by this that no one can be said to know anything about the truth of any proposition that has not underlying it a substratum of demonstratable fact. The theory of incarnation has no such basis.

Dr. James H. Hyslop, professor at Columbia University, said in 1919:

> What it is that can recommend the doctrine of reincar-

nation to its believers is difficult to understand. It contains nothing desirable and nothing ethical. ... Reincarnation is not desirable, because it does not satisfy the only instinct that makes survival interesting, namely the instinct to preserve the consciousness of personal identity. ... A future life must be the continuity of this consciousness or it is not a life to us at all. Moreover, there is nothing ethical in the doctrine. The absolutely fundamental condition of all ethics is memory and personal identity and are excluded from the processes of reincarnation.

R. Dewitt Miller in his book, *Forgotten Mysteries*, relates a peculiar experience of one Lurancy Vennum. He says:

> Lurancy Vennum, who lived with her parents in Watseka, Illinois, was a normal girl until one day in 1887, during her fourteenth year, when she suddenly fell into a profound sleep. From this she awakened as a completely new personality. The new personality said that it was that of Mary Roff, who had died twelve years before.
>
> The girl immediately took up residence with the Roff family, where she was found to have those memories which the dead girl would be expected to possess. For fifteen weeks she led the life of Mary Roff, claiming steadfastly that she had recrossed the "moment of shadow" and borrowed the body of Lurancy Vennum. And during those weeks, her every mannerism, memory, and attitude was that of the dead girl.
>
> After fifteen weeks, she said she was returning to the "other world." The girl again entered a trance-like condition. When she awakened, she was once more Lurancy Vennum.
>
> If the whole thing were some strange senseless masquerade, then Lurancy Vennum had at fourteen investigated

Mary Roff's past with a thoroughness that would do honor to the world's best secret service. There was evidence too that she possessed information which would be known only to Mary Roff.

There is no reason to believe that Mr. Miller has not gotten observational facts correct. Many similar cases have been recorded. We must take exception to his conclusions that the incident is evidence for the case of reincarnation. Such occurrences are simply the work of familiar spirits. These spirits inhabit the body of a person during their lifetime. They have opportunity naturally to learn all about the person's life, many little things that only the most intimate friends know. After their disembodiment they seek opportunity to enter another person. If and when this happens, the spirit or spirits pretend to be the spirit of the deceased. And since spiritists reject the Bible revelation of evil spirits impersonating the dead, they are ready to take their claims at face value.

The doctrine of reincarnation has had its fountain largely in Buddhism. It is at best, a hopeless teaching, clearly demonic and unscriptural. It supposes that a person goes through a long cycle of birth, life, death and then rebirth and death again and again until at last, the soul reaches a state of nirvana.

What is nirvana? It is a state of nothingness, when the soul finally dissolves into a state of unconsciousness and becomes a part of the universe; clearly this teaching is plain pantheism. It is a miserable substitute for the glorious truth of immortality revealed in the Bible.

Chapter Twenty

Sorcerers of Yesterday and Today

The study of Balaam offers enlightenment on some of the more puzzling aspects of demonic operations. It shows that there is a thin line between divine manifestations and those of Satan. He who moves into the realm of the supernatural must dedicate himself to a life of absolute obedience to the will of God, or he is in grave danger.

He who wanders onto forbidden paths lays himself open to the attacks of Satan and to delusions that can transform a person into one of the angels of light. This of course runs contrary to modern theology, which denies the existence of Satan. Nevertheless, if we are going to stand in this evil day, we must be willing to face reality.

To understand the case of Balaam correctly, we must understand that in the beginning, he indeed prophesied by the Spirit of God. Nowhere in the Old Testament are there prophecies that exceed Balaam's for beauty and poetic quality. Consider, for example, his words in Numbers 23:19-21:

> God *is* not a man, that He should lie, nor a son of man, that He should repent. Has He said, and will He not do? Or has He spoken, and will He not make it good? Behold, I have received *a command* to bless; He has blessed, and I cannot reverse it. He has not observed iniquity in Jacob,

nor has He seen wickedness in Israel. The LORD his God *is* with him, and the shout of a King *is* among them.

Or the passage in Numbers 24:16,17:

> The utterance of him who hears the words of God, and has the knowledge of the Most High, *who* sees the vision of the Almighty, *who* falls down, with eyes wide open: "I see Him, but not now; I behold Him, but not near; a Star shall come out of Jacob; a Scepter shall rise out of Israel, and batter the brow of Moab, and destroy all the sons of tumult."

Indeed we are told specifically that "the Spirit of God came upon him" (Num. 24:2) when he spake these prophecies. Unger says that nowhere is Balaam called a prophet, but Peter gives him that name although in time his folly resulted in his becoming a mad prophet (II Pet. 2:16).

To understand the case of Balaam, we must recognize his status as a prophet of Jehovah, and not just an ignorant heathen. He knew very well what he ought to do, but his trouble was that deep in his heart, he had a desire for the forbidden. For example, when Balak first sent for Balaam to curse Israel under promise to promote him to great honor, he replied, "Though Balak were to give me his house full of silver and gold, I could not go beyond the word of the LORD my God, to do less or more" (Num. 22:18).

But Balaam's weakness was his spirit of covetousness, and deep down in his heart he did want the silver and gold. God had given him an express command against going with Balak's messengers. The Lord had said, "You shall not go with them; you shall not curse the people, for they *are* blessed" (Num. 22:12).

This should have been sufficient, but Balaam was not satisfied with the directive will, but with the permissive will of God. He went to God again to see if he could cajole Him into permitting him to go with the men. And this time, God let him go. This is exactly where many people make a sad mistake. Although they have been shown a certain path, and it is not in the divine will, they desire it anyway.

Then suddenly, the way opens for them to go ahead. Mistakenly they now believe that they are moving in the divine will but actually they are on the road to disaster.

There is a thin line between true prophecy and occultism that comes from seducing spirits. Both operate in the same realm and are easily confused by the person whose principles are not oriented with the will of God. The prophet who is familiar with God's Word and adheres closely to it will quickly detect the presence of the cloven hoof. Balaam, because of his loose ethics and greed for gold and silver, soon came to the place where he could not tell the difference between divine prophecy and divination by enchantments.

Indeed in trying to earn Balak's promise of reward, he sought by enchantments to curse Israel. But in this he was checked by the Lord, who would not allow him to invoke a curse on Israel (Num. 24:1). Each time, the Spirit of the Lord came upon him so that he prophesied a blessing on Israel instead.

Balaam's playing with divining spirits was to lead to his downfall. He came to the conclusion that Israel, because of its iniquity, could be cursed. He was blind to the higher morality of a nation which had been redeemed by blood. Demon spirits are unanimous in this philosophy. Thus Balaam, speaking under the Spirit of God, said, "He has not observed iniquity in Jacob, nor has He seen wickedness in Israel" (Num. 23:21).

Because of Balaam's stubbornness, the Spirit of God left him, and he moved into a realm of divination and soothsaying. Here we see the operation of demons or seducing spirits. He finally became a toady or a paid prophet of Balak. According to Revelation 2:14, this ultimately led to enticing some of the Israelites into an immoral religious ritual and to committing fornication.

As with Saul, the Spirit of God departed from Balaam and seducing and lying spirits took its place. The prophet became a common soothsayer or fortuneteller. Joshua 13:22 tells of his untimely end.

> The children of Israel also killed with the sword Balaam the son of Beor, the soothsayer, among those who were

killed by them.

Jeane Dixon

Ruth Montgomery's book, *A Gift of Prophecy*, brought Jeane Dixon to national attention, and today her name is a household word. Many people have been led to believe that she is a prophetess in the Bible sense. However, the briefest survey of the type of operation of her "gift" immediately classifies her as a medium, howbeit a most unusually sensitive one. Apparently, it is not necessary for Mrs. Dixon to go into a trance as the average medium does (except on occasions), but she gets her revelations through psychic vibrations.

We have nothing to say against Mrs. Dixon as a woman, but there is not the slightest doubt that her "gift" is not that described by Paul in I Corinthians 12 and 14. In the first place the "gift" came at an early age after she visited a gypsy fortuneteller. She was soon able to give readings herself. She could tell fortunes, not only by means of a crystal ball which the gypsy gave her, but also by means of a deck of cards, by astrology, dreams, visions, etc. Through her psychic powers, she was able to foretell the winner of a horse race and to pick out the prize number at a raffle.

Mrs. Dixon tells how she received a vision in which she saw a great serpent twisting by the side of her bed. In the eyes of the serpent she saw "all the knowing wisdom of the ages." Now if she knew the Scriptures at all, she would have known that the serpent is none other than the devil (Rev. 20:1-3), the one who tempted Eve. The old serpent, which is the devil, is to be cast into the pit during the millennium where he will no longer have opportunity to tempt the nations:

> Then I saw an angel coming down from heaven, having the key to the bottomless pit and a great chain in his hand. He laid hold of the dragon, that serpent of old, who is *the* Devil and Satan, and bound him for a thousand years; and he cast him into the bottomless pit, and shut him up, and set a seal on him, so that he should deceive the

nations no more till the thousand years were finished. But after these things he must be released for a little while (Rev. 20:1-3).

Mrs. Dixon relates the "wisdom" that the serpent divulged to her. Among other things, it told of the coming of a great leader who will bring peace to the world. Of this man she says:

> A child, born somewhere in the Middle East shortly after 7 a.m. (EST) on February 5, 1962, will revolutionize the world. Before the close of the century he will bring together all mankind in one all-embracing faith. This will be the foundation of a new Christianity, with every sect and creed united through this man who will walk among the people to spread the wisdom of the Almighty Power. ... He is the answer to the prayers of a troubled world. Mankind will begin to feel the great force of this man in the early 1980s, and during the subsequent ten years the world as we know it will be reshaped and revamped into one without wars or suffering. His power will grow greatly until 1999, at which time the people of this earth will probably discover the full meaning of the vision!

Of course this description is not of Christ, but of the Antichrist. In our book on Jeane Dixon, we found it necessary to expose this. An Antichrist is surely coming, and he will pretend to bring peace. Instead he will drench the world in blood, as clearly depicted in Revelation 13:4-8:

> So they worshiped the dragon who gave authority to the beast; and they worshiped the beast, saying, "Who *is* like the beast? Who is able to make war with him?" And he was given a mouth speaking great things and blasphemies, and he was given authority to continue for forty-two months. Then he opened his mouth in blasphemy against God, to blaspheme His name, His tabernacle, and

those who dwell in heaven. It was granted to him to make war with the saints and to overcome them. And authority was given him over every tribe, tongue, and nation. All who dwell on the earth will worship him, whose names have not been written in the Book of Life of the Lamb slain from the foundation of the world.

Our book on Jeane Dixon attained a rather wide circulation, and apparently many people sent her a copy. Accordingly, I received a letter from her which was as follows:

Dear Mr. Lindsay:

As of today I have received yet another copy of your booklet, *The Mystery of Jeane Dixon* from friends of mine all over the country.

The "mystery" is not in my God-given talent — but in how YOU could feel qualified to publish a book of this kind when you have never met me, talked to me, interviewed me, or had a vision yourself.

You have obviously twisted the Scriptures to mean what *you* personally want them to mean ... not what *God* meant them to mean! How nice it would be if you would try to understand the Bible as it was meant to be — and not as you want it to be.

Since you are so familiar with the Scriptures, I wonder that you are not familiar with God's most perfect verse: Matthew, chapter 7, verse 1: "Judge not, that ye be not judged."

I am going to say some special prayers for you, because if you are so close to the antichrist and know all about his coming, I feel you need them very badly.

Blessings unlimited,

Jeane L. Dixon

Since I had nothing against the woman herself, I wrote her the following reply, requesting that since she thought that I misunderstood her teachings, I would be happy to meet with her and have her show me that her ministry was in line with the Scriptures. The letter was as follows:

> Dear Mrs. Dixon:
>
> I received your letter today and have carefully read the contents.
>
> I believe that if you read my book carefully, you found that I in no way spoke against you, but regarded you as a woman of character and one that was quite sincere in what you are doing.
>
> In your letter you complain that I have never met you nor talked with you nor interviewed you, and I assume from that you have information to give me that might cause me to modify or change my views. I should be quite willing to meet with you and to give you opportunity to point out the things which you feel I have misinterpreted or given an incorrect representation. I would also be pleased to have you show me the Scriptures which you think that I have twisted.
>
> Again I say that I think you are a sincere woman and I wish to give you this opportunity to correct anything that is not in line with the Scriptures. With best wishes, I am
>
> Sincerely yours,
>
> Gordon Lindsay

I never received any reply to this. But there was one surprising result. Mrs. Dixon put out another book completely reversing the first and admitting that the man she first said was going to bring peace to the world was actually the Antichrist! And the serpent which had given her the great wisdom recorded in the first was actually the devil!

Arthur Ford

Any discussion of spiritism should include a few paragraphs about Arthur Ford. Mr. Ford, who is now deceased, was perhaps the world's best known medium. His powers attracted the attention of leading spiritualists such as Sir Arthur Conan Doyle, Sir Oliver Lodge, Sir William Crookes and others. There is no doubt that Ford's psychic powers rivaled those of any other medium of his time.

Arthur Ford was christened in an Episcopal church. His mother was a Baptist. In his early years, he attended Sunday school and church. But he soon developed a deep antagonism for any preaching that included mention of hell. He states in his book, *Nothing So Strange*, that he played the piano for the young people's service and even joined the Baptist church. But when he reached the age of 15, he came upon some booklets written by a unitarian minister, one of which was entitled, *Evolution and Religion*. These books apparently shook what little faith the young man had. When the elders of the church found he was circulating these books among the congregation, his name was removed from the roll of the Baptist church.

Having left the faith of his mother, he became interested in psychic literature. Before long, he found that he himself was psychic. He became acquainted with a professor who was interested in spiritualism, and young Ford soon became absorbed in the phenomena of occultism and mysticism. He now associated prayer with clairvoyance and clairaudience. He also discovered that unholy persons could exercise psychic gifts. The spirits themselves were immoral.

Ford moved from one kind of psychic phenomenon to another, including hypnotism, ESP, spiritist demonstrations and others. He attempted to make contacts with spirits during the séances. At first, he had rather limited success. But then he found the secret — laying himself completely open to the spirits. He said: "I found that my main task on such occasions *was to make myself open to whatever might come though.*"

But then he found that the spirit realm became congested with spirit entities, each one clamoring for an audience. What to do? His problem was solved when a "guide" came and took command of the situation. This master of ceremonies restored order, permitting only one spirit to speak at a time. Ford called him his "partner and right-hand man." Just as godly people have guardian angels (Matt. 18:10), so apparently those in league with the devil have guardian demons.

And thus Ford found himself able to carry on séances that astonished the unwary and those uninstructed in the Scriptures. This "guide" acted as an intermediary between people and their "deceased relatives," which were, however, none other than impersonating spirits.

Ford soon found that there were no moral requirements at all to spiritualism. He became a drug addict and an alcoholic. His second wife put up with him as long as she could and then divorced him. In recalling his experience he said, "It was almost as if an invading entity had taken over, worked his havoc and left when satiated." He was not far wrong. There are demons of drink that destroy the personality and lead to the hideous experience of delirium tremens in which a person sees snakes, bugs, demons with bulging eyes, etc. Drunkenness is one of the many curses of spiritism. The founders of modern spiritualism, the Fox sisters, in their last days, as we have said, degenerated into human derelicts who went to drunkards' graves.

Spiritualism led Ford into a belief in reincarnation. Certainly the Bible utterly denies this teaching: "It is appointed for men to die once, but after this the judgment" (Heb. 9:27). The teachings of spiritualism have nothing whatever in common with Christianity.

In one of his trances Ford supposedly saw "judges" in the spirit realm. He noted, "Their categories of sin were not those of the Baptist church of my youth — alcoholism, sex, and what are called worldly pursuits. Rather they spoke of failure to use the energy gifts opportunities." When Ford met them, he went into a tantrum, according to his account, and gave them a sound cursing. Then he came out of his trance. Clearly the spiritualism that Ford knew was a fellowship of demons (I Cor. 10:20).

Mrs. Tweedale's Psychic Powers

As we have said, those engaged in what they term "psychic research" generally rule out the scriptural explanation of occult manifestations as being demonic manifestations. Some consider the demonstrations a special form of psychic energy emanating from the certain types of individuals. More frequently, mediums or sensitives, consider this phenomenon as produced by the spirits of the dead. They do differentiate between spirits, for they explain that just as there are good and bad living people, naturally when people die, some are good and bad. With rare exceptions, they do not concede that these spirits are demons, and they utterly reject the idea that they are unwittingly in league with the devil. This is understandable, for did they believe this, they would seek to be loosed from the power of these spirits. Occasionally, a medium who is a sincere seeker after truth will become aware of the true nature of the spirits and seek deliverance. Then he finds that he has a terrific battle, for the spirits have no desire to lose control over the victims that they have been able to dupe in the past.

Some people are extremely sensitive to psychic powers. Such persons should be exceedingly careful not to play with any form of psychic phenomena such as ESP, telepathy, Ouija board or divining of any kind since once under bondage to these spirits, they will find it exceedingly difficult to get loose. Edgar Cayce, the famous psychic, tried desperately to be freed from his divining powers, being convinced they were demonic. Unable to free himself, he gave up and devoted his life to occultism.

One of the more famous psychics was a Scotswoman by the name of Violet Tweedale, a crusader for women's rights and a political activist. In her book, *Ghosts I Have Seen*, she relates a vast number of psychic experiences, ranging from séances to seeing ghosts, apparitions and experimenting in occultism of every kind. Her father had a great interest in the preternatural, and the daughter, no doubt for this reason, became predisposed to venture into the psychic realms.

Even as a child, she had experiences of this kind. She tells that at the age of 6, before drifting off to sleep at bedtime, she and her brother would hear footsteps going up the double flight of stairs, accompanied by the rustling of silken skirts. No person was ever seen nor did the children ever hear the unseen walker go downstairs. In the morning, they would awaken to an absolute pandemonium of noise, as if the furniture were being thrown around, then things would quiet down.

At the age of 20, Mrs. Tweedale abandoned orthodox religion. She was attracted to the notorious Elena Petrovna Blavatsky, founder of theosophy, an occult religion marked by the most radical demonic delusions. Madam Blavatsky was a commanding personage, and Mrs. Tweedale was easily lured into belief in her peculiar doctrines of reincarnation and karma.

Following this, she began to delve deeply into spiritualism and soon discovered that she too was a medium. She began her operations with the Ouija board, continuing for some time until the spirits showed her other more direct methods of communication.

She then discovered she had power to see ghosts. These ghosts usually had a relation to some wicked person who had died, who perhaps had committed a violent crime. The demons that survived the death seemed to have obtained an affinity for the house where the evil took place.

On one occasion, she met an alcoholic ghost. Her psychic attention was drawn to a gray cloud hovering in a corner of the room. The mist gradually took the form of a small attractive woman offering her a drink of whiskey. Upon investigation, she learned that a woman had died in that place of extreme alcoholism. She believed that this was the spirit of the woman. Of course, the true explanation was that the apparition or spirit was the demon that had possessed the woman.

Later in her life, these apparitions began to appear in a more frightening manner. Previously she had taken the visitations as a matter of course. One particular apparition of a man staring into a fire alarmed her. The ghost appeared so often that finally her nerves were almost shattered. She claims that a Franciscan monk helped to free her from the apparition.

Mrs. Tweedale related other strange experiences. She awakened one night while traveling in Bohemia to see a dozen nonhuman creatures playing leapfrog around her room. As she watched them, she saw the three-foot bodies surmounted by heads of apes.

In her later years, she would have horrifying nightmares. Once she dreamed she had committed murder and was attempting to hide the corpse in a secret place. While in the act, she was discovered by a gentleman entering the front hallway. The horror climaxed in a white cloud, at which time she awoke. This dream recurred again and again over many years.

She also possessed powers similar to Jeane Dixon and could pick out winners of horse races. Modern psychic research glibly explains it all as psychic phenomena. The Bible declares it to be sorcery and witchcraft.

Bishop Pike and the Seducing Spirits

One of the saddest stories of modern times is that of Bishop Pike. Brought up in the Catholic church, he became disillusioned with the concept of papal infallibility. During his college years, he professed to be an atheist. Later he turned back to religion and joined the Episcopal church. His rise was rapid as an Episcopal priest. Within a few years, he was made dean of St. John the Divine, the world's largest cathedral. In time, he became recognized as one of the world's leading spokesmen of Christianity.

Seducing spirits saw in Bishop Pike an opportunity to strike a master blow against Christianity. He suddenly announced to the world he no longer believed in the virgin birth. His descent into apostasy was rapid. One by one, he repudiated the fundamental teachings of the Word of God. He was charged with heresy by the Episcopal House of Bishops and was censured.

Now the bishop began to disintegrate as a man. He mocked the faith he once preached. He led the van of the defiant in an effort to overthrow the establishment. He left the Episcopal church to go his own way. It remained for history to render a verdict as to whether his course brought peace to his soul or tragedy to his life. The world did not have long to wait. Bishop Pike had no inkling that the spirits that had led him from his faith would soon destroy his home. His son, Jim, began to lose all direction in life. He became critical of everything. Soon the youth began failing in his studies. He went to the psychiatrists, but they could not help him. He became withdrawn and uncommunicative, evidence of demon spirits closing in.

The psychiatrist suggested a trip on LSD, and the father acquiesced. Months went by, and Jim's health began to decline. Since the bishop renounced his faith, it was not surprising that the son did also. He joined the hippies and continued using drugs. Going into a deep trance, he would say, "It's a dark road, and getting darker as I am along it."

The father tried to rehabilitate the lad, but the son said, "I'm falling into nothingness ... no way to grab hold ... save me, save. ..." A few days later, the tormented son took a gun and shot himself.

Bishop Pike, having lost his faith, had no hope of life beyond the grave. He could not believe the Bible, but he was wide open to delusions of seducing spirits. A series of bizarre occurrences took place in his home.

Mysterious objects began to fly around the house. His secretary had strange experiences. The bishop was convinced that his dead son was in some way connected with these peculiar manifestations. Like Saul of old, he decided to visit a witch — a person who today is called a spiritualist medium. The medium brought his "son" up. "Jim" explained that he was not in purgatory. He congratulated the bishop on the book he was writing which purported to reveal to the world the true religion versus Christianity.

In the midst of this confusion, his secretary, Marin Bergrud, who had become a full-fledged spiritualist, committed suicide. The bishop met with Allen Spragget, a psychic who had turned from a Bible faith to spiritualism. On a television program scheduled by Spragget, Pike had a long conversation with a spirit purported to be that of his dead son. People warned the bishop that the spirit that was talking to him was not his son, but a familiar spirit. Leviticus

19:31 was quoted to him. He impatiently waved all this aside.

The bishop adopted a new morality that permitted adultery under certain circumstances. Upon this, his wife, Esther Pike, could take no more and terminated the marriage. The bishop married his new secretary, Diane Kennedy. Together, they made a trip to the Judean desert in search of the historical Christ. Out in the wilderness, they lost their way. Diane went for help. When searchers were alerted, they found the bishop had disappeared. They consulted Arthur Ford, the famous medium, for directions. He told the searchers that the bishop was alive in a cave. His information, as it proved out, came from lying spirits. Six days later, the bishop was found, not in a cave. He was in a kneeling position, but life had long departed.

Surely Bishop Pike is an object lesson to those who depart from the faith and give heed to seducing spirits. Shortly after, Arthur Ford also died. Both men, victims of seducing spirits, at last came to the hour of truth.

What further need we say? Demonology is an unpleasant subject. Yet we cannot avoid it, for millions of people are becoming involved in its toils, soon to become slaves of tormenting spirits. As we have shown, the Bible has given solemn warnings against all psychic manifestations, including sorcery and occultism in their various garbs. All these are the operation of demon spirits whose sole objective is first to secure a body to dwell in, and secondly, to lead the person they have snared into delusion and eternal death.

Therefore, let everyone who has dallied in any way with these occult practices turn from them as they would a plague. Instead, let them look to Jesus, "the author and finisher of *our* faith" (Heb. 12:2). He will satisfy the innermost longing of the soul, and there will be no need of experimenting with spirits for whom is reserved as their portion the night of everlasting darkness.

Part V:

Gaining Dominion Over Satan and His Cohorts

Chapter Twenty-One

How Demons Gain Control

In order to understand our subject properly, we must first learn how and under what circumstances demons are able to gain control of a person. Obviously these malicious spirits cannot at will take possession of an individual, else all would soon become demon possessed. Something, therefore, must happen that breaks down the natural barriers that God has set up to keep demons from obtaining entrance. (The King James Version uses the term "devils," other versions use the word "demons." For practical purposes the two words are interchangeable.)

It is, therefore, of paramount importance to understand how demons enter in the first place, for if the door of entrance is not kept closed, there is a good chance that they will return. For this reason, teaching is important before prayer is made for those seeking deliverance from demonic oppression so that proper precautions may be taken to prevent a recurrence of the condition.

The matter of demonic activity is not one to be taken lightly. The torment of malicious spirits is a most excruciating experience, and should demons get full control of a person, they can reduce him to a state of torment and despair. Alas, many people choose to dally with these spirits, not realizing that they are sowing seeds that can lead to a harvest of woe. Let us, therefore, begin by considering how evil powers can break through the normal defenses and enter the human body which God had intended to be the temple of the Holy Ghost.

The Story of King Saul

A study of the life of Saul affords the best example in the Scriptures of how a demon or demons gradually take control of a person. Young Saul was not a disadvantaged person, who, because of environment and poverty, became subject to evil influences. The Scriptures introduce him in most favorable terms. "And he had a choice and handsome son whose name *was* Saul. *There was* not a more handsome person than he among the children of Israel. From his shoulders upward *he was* taller than any of the people" (I Sam. 9:2). Saul obviously had what is called today "charisma," that rather hard-to-define quality that attracts and hold friends. He looked every bit of a king, and he was a king.

The first chapters that deal with his story present a rather attractive account of his qualities as a man. At the time, he was crowned king, he showed a commendable humility, and he certainly did not put himself forward in any way. Nor did he after he became king seek reprisal or revenge against those who had opposed him, though there were those who counseled him otherwise. He declared, "Not a man shall be put to death this day, for today the LORD has accomplished salvation in Israel" (I Sam. 11:13).

Nor was Saul a man without a definite experience with the Lord. After Samuel had anointed him, the prophet said, "Then the Spirit of the LORD will come upon you, and you will prophesy with them and be turned into another man" (I Sam. 10:6).

In spite of these favorable circumstances, there were certain indications that all was not as well as it should be. Saul appeared to have an inner feeling of insecurity which made him suspicious of anyone who might prove a rival to him. His family also seemed to have a strange lack of piety, insomuch that when the Spirit of the Lord came upon Saul, his friends were so taken by surprise that they exclaimed, "*Is* Saul also among the prophets?" (I Sam. 10:12).

There was another weakness in Saul. He was inclined to be impetuous, given to acting on sudden impulse. This was clearly evidenced at Gilgal. When Samuel failed to arrive as soon as expected, the king usurped authority for offering the sacrifice which God reserved only for the priesthood. Saul also was inclined to give way under pressure, and on occasion, disobeyed the explicit commandments of the Lord. Thus he spared King Agag and the best of the flocks, although God has given him a commission to extirpate the Amalekites, a people given to extreme wickedness. When Samuel confronted him with his failure to carry out orders, he squirmed and laid the blame on the people.

Saul's acts of disobedience brought condemnation from the prophet Samuel. But instead of correcting his conduct, he sulked over what he thought was his bad luck, and this brooding opened the way to the dark powers. A sort of melancholia settled upon the king, a spirit of depression which is an unmistakable sign that evil spirits have begun their work.

In each human heart there is a spiritual void which will be filled with God's presence as divinely intended, or else it gradually becomes the habitation of evil spirits. So it was in the case of Saul. Finally the Spirit of the Lord departed from him, and that place was usurped by an evil spirit (I Sam. 16:14).

The servants of the king correctly discerned Saul's condition as demonic, and suggested that David, a youth upon whom the Spirit of God rested, minister to him with the hope that the king might receive deliverance. When evil spirits of oppression first begin to afflict a person, right then is the time to take action before their hold gets too strong. When David ministered to Saul by playing on his harp, and perhaps singing some of his psalms, the evil spirit would depart:

> And so it was, whenever the spirit from God was upon Saul, that David would take a harp and play *it* with his hand. Then Saul would become refreshed and well, and the distressing spirit would depart from him (I Sam. 16:23).

All unsaved persons suffer a measure of oppression by the enemy (II Tim. 2:25,26). But when they come in contact with a Spirit-filled individual or group, it is not unusual for them to be greatly affected — some more than others. If they yield to the call of the Spirit and repent of their sins, the devil's power over them is broken. "Therefore if the Son makes you free, you shall be free indeed" (Jn. 8:36).

But as Jesus solemnly declared, it is necessary afterward to walk with the Lord. "If you abide in My word, you are My disciples indeed" (Jn. 8:31). Disobedience to known light or yielding to carnal passions can erode away the blessing and result in the return of the evil spirit with possibly additional ones (Lk. 11:24-26). In that case, the person's state is worse than it was before.

And so it proved with Saul. Although he received deliverance, he failed to profit by it and continued to be governed by his elemental passions. Envy and jealousy were his besetting sins and largely the cause of his downfall. Suspicious of the motives of David, he became obsessed with the idea that David was after his throne. As Saul continued to brood over these things, the evil spirit — evidently a murderous one — took possession of him, and he began to make attempts on the life of David:

> And it happened on the next day that the distressing spirit from God came upon Saul, and he prophesied inside the house. So David played *music* with his hand, as at other times; but *there was* a spear in Saul's hand. And Saul cast the spear, for he said, "I will pin David to the wall!" But David escaped his presence twice (I Sam. 18:10,11).

What a warning to those who fail to curb their passions! While it is not always sinful to be angry, the Apostle Paul said, "Do not let the sun go down on your wrath" (Eph. 4:26). By failing in this respect, people provide an open door for evil spirits to gain dominion. Nevertheless, in Saul's case the control of the enemy was not yet absolute. If a person attacked by Satan awakes to his danger, he can through repentance and resistance against the enemy be rescued from his peril.

Saul, however, by his self-will and failure to profit by his mistakes, was on a headlong course for disaster. Nevertheless, God gave him one more chance. David had fled from Saul after Saul had attempted to kill him, and he went to Samuel. Together they went to live at Naioth for rest and safety. When Saul heard David was with Samuel, he sent troops to capture him. But the Spirit of God came upon them, and they began prophesying. Saul had sent a second group, and a third; but all were overcome by the Spirit and forgot their mission. Finally, Saul himself went after David. As he drew near Naioth, the Spirit of God came upon him, and he, too, began to prophesy:

> So he went there to Naioth in Ramah. Then the Spirit of God was upon his also, and he went on and prophesied until he came to Naioth in Ramah. And he also stripped off his clothes and prophesied before Samuel in like manner, and lay down naked all that day and all that night. Therefore they say, "*Is* Saul also among the prophets?" (I Sam. 19:23,24).

Thus we see that God in His mercy and compassion gave Saul another opportunity to obtain deliverance — one more respite before the devil closed the trap. Saul came under the power of the Spirit of God, but the demons had gained such control that they were contesting fiercely. It was no doubt the struggle within him between good and evil that caused him to tear the very clothes from his back, and lie on the ground through the day and night.

Had Saul learned his lesson and chosen to retain his deliverance, it could have been the turning point in his life. But jealousy and self-will had such a hold upon him that he turned inward to his passions and thereby forged the chains of his doom. From then on, Saul was paranoid. He lived in a state of delusion that David was trying to kill him, even though the latter twice spared his life when he could have taken it. Nothing could shake his obsession, and it drove him on relentlessly. Should anyone stand in his way, including his own son, Jonathan, this murderous spirit within Saul sought to kill him.

In an insane rage, he ordered the death of the priests who had innocently inquired of the Lord for David. From that time on, there was no answer when Saul prayed. He finally consulted with a witch, who warned him of his impending doom. Saul's last act was that of suicide.

The story of the king's backsliding and opening himself to the control of evil spirits is one that has been repeated many times. His sad end was the inevitable fruit of self-will — the habitual yielding to his own passions.

The Bible reveals what really takes place behind the scenes, which psychiatrists as a rule do not understand. The backslider who drifts away from God becomes subject to the activities of malicious spirits which have no other purpose than to reduce their hapless victim to the permanent state of depravity they are in.

As we have noted, people without Christ gradually come under the sway of evil powers. In most cases, they do not actually become demon possessed or even obsessed, but their disinclination to spiritual things deepens. And the call of the Spirit becomes weaker and weaker. This may occur in a short while, or in some cases, over a long period of time.

Certain activities can bring them quickly under the power of evil spirits. Trifling with or trafficking in any kind of spiritualism is a sure way. I recall the case of a woman who was on the point of a nervous breakdown because years before, she had indulged in attempting contact with the spirits. In this she was far more successful than she intended, for being sensitive to psychic influences, evil spirits got a lodging place in her mind and would not leave. They were of the chattering kind that babbled much of the time, mostly nonsense. This torment of voices went on ceaselessly year after year.

She came to us one day for ministry. We told her that in order to receive deliverance and keep it, she must break away from friends who were responsible for leading her into that condition. She told us these friends had warned her not to have anything to do with Full Gospel people. She did not know whether she could break away from them or not. We told her frankly that her deliverance was at stake, and she would have to make that choice. We prayed with her, and we believed deliverance was on the threshold, but whether she was fully delivered or not, we cannot say, for we never saw her again.

Time and again, we have met people troubled with talking spirits. Invariably they have had a past history of dallying with the occult. It is so easy for these demons to get control and so difficult to get free from them that we can only warn people in most solemn terms to flee from them as they would the plague to avoid years of misery and torment.

Victor H. Ernest, who was for a time a devotee of spiritualism, tells in his book, *I Talked With Spirits,* of the battle he had with demons after he was converted and became a minister. He says, "My conversion to Christ from spiritualism occurred in 1929, but I was not free from demon interference for many years after I entered the pastorate. The influence of demonism continued strong among my relatives. ... I never preached on demonism in my own church, except when the subject came up in my regular sermons. But when other churches had me speak on demonism in special meetings, the demons I had once welcomed into my body in séances attacked my mind and vocal chords.

"Sometimes my memory would go blank; other times my throat would constrict, and I couldn't speak. As soon as I prayed for help, through the power of Jesus' blood the attack ceased and I continued. These assaults continued sporadically for thirteen years before my spiritual defenses were built up to keep demons from penetrating my body. As my spiritual armor became strong, I was able to help others assailed by spirits."

Such testimonies given by men who have fully consecrated their lives to God are certainly a warning to those who dabble in spirits. The victims, even after their eyes are opened to the true nature of their unholy visitors, are usually ill-prepared to battle months and even years against the spirits who insist on returning. When the divine barrier against these malicious demons is broken down, it is not easy to restore it to its original condition.

As we have said, God has so formed the human body that it has natural resistance against demons, just as it resists the invasion of disease germs. Should alien bacteria enter the bloodstream of a person, immediately the white corpuscles mobilize to block and destroy the invader, another example of the forethought of the Creator. In this same way, the body has natural defenses against demonic intrusion. Evil spirits may oppress sinners, but except the door is opened in some way, demons cannot enter and take full possession.

But there is another opening of which demons take advantage. God's protection is promised to His people who daily look to Him. Psalm 91 contains wonderful promises of God's watchful care over those who dwell "in the secret place of the Most High." We are told that they "shall abide under the shadow of the Almighty" (vs. 1).

This has been proven by multitudes of faithful believers. But what about marginal Christians — professing Christians who have never really learned what it means to "walk with God"? They have not entered into that realm of rest spoken of in Psalm 91. In case of accident or misadventure, they do not live close enough to Him to enjoy this special protection.

Demons Are Not to be Trifled With

It is one thing to be oppressed of Satan; it is a much worse thing to be demon possessed. And some of these demons are exceedingly tenacious. It is a fact that certain demons are much more powerful than others. Demons in a way are like people; they vary greatly in strength and power. This was clearly indicated by Jesus Himself.

The disciples apparently had remarkable success in casting out demons (Lk. 10:17), and their confidence increased until they were ready to take on almost any case. Nevertheless, while Jesus was on the Mount of Transfiguration, a man brought his son for deliverance who was possessed of a powerful epileptic demon. When the disciples tried to cast it out, they were unsuccessful (Mk. 9:14-29). However, when Jesus came on the scene, the demon had to go. The disciples were puzzled, and when they were apart from the company, they asked the Lord, "Why could we not cast it out?" (Mk. 1:28). The Lord replied, "This kind can come out by nothing but prayer and fasting" (Mk. 9:29).

From this it is clear that some demons are far more obstinate than others. Before they can be exorcised, there must be prayer and fasting. That does not mean that prayer and fasting must precede each deliverance. In the case of Jesus, He had already done His fasting and was prepared to meet the devil; the demon had to go at once. But certainly fasting is an important element in the successful casting out of demons.

It is clear that casting out devils involves more than chanting the Name of Jesus. Truly it is in that Name that the devils have to go. But unless the command is given by one anointed by the Spirit, the words are mere syllables; for Jesus said that He cast out demons by the Spirit of God (Matt. 12:28). It is dangerous to attempt to drive out these spirits without the anointing of God. This is well-illustrated in the case of the sons of Sceva:

> Then some of the itinerant Jewish exorcists took it upon themselves to call the name of the Lord Jesus over those who had evil spirits, saying, "We exorcise you by the Jesus whom Paul preaches." Also there were seven sons of Sceva, a Jewish chief priest, who did so. And the evil spirit answered and said, "Jesus I know, and Paul I know; but who are you?" Then the man in whom the evil spirit was leaped on them, overpowered them, and prevailed against them, so that they fled out of that house naked and wounded (Acts 19:13-16).

Casting Out Demons is a Practical Matter

The casting out of devils is an important and a very practical matter. For today, as well as in past millenniums, millions of people have been or are being oppressed and tormented by demons.

In the Old Testament, little is recorded about the casting out of demons. The people of those days knew almost nothing about Satan except that he existed and controlled a vast army of evil spirits intent upon injuring the human race. The righteous looked forward to the coming of the Messiah (Jn. 4:25), Who would reveal all things to His people, and Who would deliver the earth from Satan's curse.

Satan secured a lease, as it were, on God's fair creation, and since the fall of Adam, has influenced its affairs more or less as he pleased. In delivering the children of Israel from Egypt and bringing them into covenant relationship with Him, God intended to not only release them from the Egyptian taskmasters, but also from Satan's dominion (Pharaoh was a type of Satan). God's redeemed people were to be free. Unfortunately, the children of Israel disobeyed the Law and broke the covenant. As a result, they lost their independence, coming under the rule of gentile nations, which in turn were under the dominion of the powers of darkness.

The activity of evil spirits is recorded in numerous places in the Old Testament. Usually it was disobedience to God which made the individual vulnerable to the evil spirits. Such was the case with Saul, the first king of Israel. When the Spirit of the Lord left Saul, an evil spirit came upon him. "But the Spirit of the LORD departed from Saul, and a distressing spirit from the LORD troubled him" (I Sam. 16:14). We cannot avoid the significance of this statement. People are faced with two alternatives: They must serve either God or the devil. One or the other will ultimately be their master.

It is apparent that Saul did not become completely demon possessed, but was oppressed by an evil spirit that gradually increased its grip upon him. It is significant to note that in the early stages of Saul's malady, the devil had only a comparatively mild hold upon him. When David played songs of praise on his harp in Saul's presence, the evil spirit left him. "And so it was, whenever the spirit from God was upon Saul, that David would take a harp and play *it* with his hand. Then Saul would become refreshed and well, and the distressing spirit would depart from him" (I Sam. 16:23). This statement is enlightening.

When sinners enter the house of God and their heart is open to the worship, they will be deeply affected by the gospel songs and message. The oppressing spirits will leave for a time, and if the person does not resist the conviction of the Spirit, he will become converted to Christ and freed from the dominion of Satan (II Tim. 2:26). If Saul had been sincere, he would have been liberated from the power of the evil spirit for all time. But because he continued in his self-will and nourished his jealous spirit, the demon returned to plague him and lead him down the road to ruin.

Those who sense real freedom in the house of the Lord only to be in bondage when they leave may be experiencing demonic oppression. They need to take authority over these spirits.

Chapter Twenty-Two

Testing for the Presence of Evil Spirits

> Beloved, do not believe every spirit, but test the spirits, whether they are of God; because many false prophets have gone out into the world. By this you know the Spirit of God: Every spirit that confesses that Jesus Christ has come in the flesh is of God, and every spirit that does not confess that Jesus Christ has come in the flesh is not of God. And this is the *spirit* of the Antichrist, which you have heard was coming, and is now already in the world (I Jn. 4:1-3).

Obviously, before we can cast out evil spirits, we must be able to discern between demonic activities and the manifestations of the Spirit of God. There are times when the operations of evil powers closely counterfeit or imitate those which are of God.

The Scriptures have given us certain tests by which we can determine if a spirit is of God or is false. It is the devil's policy to hide his true identity whenever possible, and pose as a messenger of God. Notwithstanding, it is not possible for a demon to conceal all its marks, and a person who is familiar with the Scriptures should have little difficulty in identifying its operations.

An evil spirit is often able to simulate closely the work of the Holy Spirit. In the case of Aaron whose rod turned into a serpent, the magicians were able to imitate the miracle (Ex. 7:10-12). Evidently God purposely recorded this incident so that we will be on the alert not to suppose that everything supernatural is of God. For indeed, myriads of people today are doing that very thing and are being led into grievous delusions.

How different the outcome would have been if Eve had been able to discern behind the smooth talk of the serpent was the tongue of God's archenemy, Satan. No doubt she would have fled in stark horror. The mistake that led to her downfall was allowing doubt to enter her heart concerning the veracity of God's words. The serpent did not call God a liar outright, but in a subtle insinuation cast doubt on His words: "Has God indeed said?" (Gen. 3:1). How often are people led into delusion by dallying with the devil's suggestions, rather than standing upon "thus says the Lord."

When any spirit, regardless of its claims, casts doubt on the Word, it is not of God. One day, I heard a certain man being interviewed on a news telecast. He is engaged in establishing homosexual churches. The newscaster asked him about the Scriptures in both the Old Testament and the New Testament that denounce in strong terms those who practice these things (Rom. 1:24-32). The man replied that he was concerned only with the words of Jesus. But he utterly ignored Jesus' words: "O foolish ones, and slow of heart to believe in all that the prophets have spoken!" (Lk. 24:25). Such people are totally deceived by lying spirits. When people reconcile Christianity with the vilest of practices, there is little hope short of a miracle of their extricating themselves.

Jeane Dixon considers herself a prophetess of the order described in I Corinthians 12. But for years, she published a daily syndicated astrology column in the newspapers, notwithstanding that the Word of God severely condemns the practice.

> Let now the astrologers, the stargazers, *and* the monthly prognosticators stand up and save you from what shall come upon you. Behold, they shall be as stubble, the fire shall burn them; they shall not deliver themselves from the power of the flame; it *shall* not *be* a coal to be warmed

by, *nor* a fire to sit before! (Isa. 47:13,14).

Over the years, she has made many statements which are wholly unscriptural. Why? Because she listens to false spirits rather than the Word of God. She calls them psychic vibrations, but they are the mouthings of demons which cleverly conceal their identity.

The test of any teaching must be whether or not it conforms to the Word of God. But people get carried away with some fascinating personality and ignore altogether whether his or her teaching is in harmony with the Scriptures. This is the way cults and false religions originate. Many people who should know better blunder into darkness because they listen to a false spirit.

I remember some years ago, a lady prophesied in a service that if the people would pray all night for a certain blind individual, the person would be healed. They came and prayed all through the night. Nothing happened. The lady had a false spirit which wanted to throw reproach on the truth of divine healing. All-night prayer meetings have great value, but people are healed through faith and not because someone prays a certain length of time.

Referring again to Jeane Dixon, while some of her prophecies have come true, many have not. She predicted war with China. She predicted that Richard Nixon would win over John Kennedy in the 1960 presidential election. Now these predictions cannot be classified the same as those made on the basis of pure human judgment, which admittedly is fallible. But if one claims that the revelation is of God, it must come to pass or it is not of God. Here is the scriptural test:

> And if you say in your heart, "How shall we know the word which the LORD has not spoken?" — when a prophet speaks in the name of the LORD, if the thing does not happen or come to pass, that *is* the thing which the LORD has not spoken; the prophet has spoken it presumptuously; you shall not be afraid of him (Deut. 18:21,22).

Psychics, in order to excuse their blunders, now are following the plan of weather forecasters — there's a 50 percent, 30 percent or 10 percent chance. These persons hedge their predictions by saying they are 60 percent correct, 70 percent, etc. Since many predictions can be guessed at with 50 percent accuracy, either the psychics are merely making shrewd guesses, or their prognostications come from lying spirits.

A seducing spirit by its nature must lie. It cannot speak at length without making at least some false statements. These spirits often profess to give out a new revelation, a new teaching. Sometimes they call it a "deeper truth." It may be a new revelation of deity or a new mode of water baptism (there have been over 20 different teachings on water baptism). Often these teachings contain partial truth with a dangerous element of error. Satan, in seeking to tempt Christ, once quoted (or rather, misquoted) Scripture to Him. Often a false religion may be tested by reason of its denial, either directly or indirectly, of the deity of Christ. An evil spirit will generally distort the truth of Christ's deity in some way, such as denying the virgin birth or affirming that Jesus was a created being, or that He was only a perfect human.

Christian Science, for example, denies that there is anything physical at all; therefore, Christ could not have come in the flesh. Other cults — unitarianism, universalism, Jehovah's Witnesses, modernism, Christadelphianism, New Thought, etc. — believe Jesus came in the flesh, but they do not believe He is the Christ; they deny His deity. Their teachings owe their origin and perpetuation through the action of seducing spirits.

Jesus gave still another test whereby we can determine whether a person is of God or not. He said, "You will know them by their fruits" (Matt. 7:16). Paul, who spoke in tongues more than all (I Cor. 14:18), informed us that speaking with tongues without love is meaningless noise like a loud gong or a clanging cymbal. He said that a knowledge of all mysteries is useless without love. Even a willingness to give away one's fortune or to become a martyr, if not motivated by love, profits nothing (I Cor. 13:1-3).

In the light of this test, it would seem that many professing Christians, including leaders, would have a difficult time in making a passing grade. Divine gifts are certainly a token of God's presence, but they are not a final proof. Certainly Balaam had the true gift of prophecy, but he wound up his unhappy career as a soothsayer, and died under the judgment of God. Apparently, the Spirit of God departed from him, and a spirit of divination took over.

There is a gift of the Spirit which discerns whether spirits are true or false. There are those whose ministry brings them in contact with false spirits. When Paul was preaching in the city of Philippi, a girl possessed with a divination spirit tried to pose as an advocate of the Gospel and cried out, "These men are the servants of the Most High God, who proclaim to us the way of salvation" (Acts 16:17). Paul discerned it to be a false demonic spirit and cast it out, though it got him and his companion Silas into considerable trouble. The gift enables persons to discern true spirits. Elisha prayed that the young man who was with him would have his eyes opened to see the hosts of angels that were protecting them from the enemy. The gift's most beneficial function, however, is in discerning evil spirits which seek to pose as the Holy Spirit.

While we were holding meetings in the South years ago, many were getting saved and receiving the baptism of the Spirit. Young people would go off in groups to pray, and often one of them would receive the Holy Spirit. On one occasion, one of the young men working with me was with a group when suddenly a young girl began to prophesy. But the prophesying took a peculiar turn. She began to recite in detail some of the acts of the young minister while he was still a sinner. He was so embarrassed that he fell to the ground in a faint. This was reported to me, and I immediately said it was the word of an evil spirit. Once sins are under the blood, the Holy Spirit never brings them up again. They are blotted out. God has forgotten them, and we should also. The girl was prayed for, and the spirit rebuked.

Victor Ernest, a Baptist minister who was a spiritist medium in his early adulthood, gives in his book, *I Talked With Spirits*, a most interesting account. Becoming a little doubtful of spiritualism, he began to read the Bible: "Beloved, do not believe every spirit, but test the spirits, whether they are of God; because many false prophets have gone out into the world" (I Jn. 4:1). Much impressed by this admonition, he determined to make the test. At the next séance, the control spirit announced that it would be a question and answer session. So when it was his turn to ask a question, he asked the spirit if it believed that Jesus was the Son of God.

The spirit passed this over smoothly by saying, "Of course, my child, Jesus is the Son of God. Only believe as the Bible says." This rather surprised Mr. Ernest, for in other séances he had heard that Jesus was a great medium and was an advanced spirit now in one of the higher planes.

So he asked the spirit, "Do you believe that Jesus Christ is the Savior of the world?" Instead of answering the question directly, the spirit said, "My child, why do you doubt? Why do you not believe? You have been this long time with us; why do you continue to doubt?" The spirit began to quote Scriptures on believing.

Once more Mr. Ernest's turn for a question came around, and this time he decided to put it plainly. He said, "O spirit, do you believe that Jesus is the Son of God, that He is the Savior of the world, that Jesus died on the cross and shed His blood for the remission of sin?"

The medium, deep in a trance, was thrown off his chair, and falling on the floor, lay groaning as if in deep pain. The sounds that came were heard as bedlam and confusion. The séance was broken up, and it took some time and much massaging of the pulse areas before the medium was revived. Then Mr. Ernest knew that these spirits were not of God. He never again attended a séance, and shortly after, was truly converted to Christ.

Summary of the Habits of Demons

From the Scriptures, certain facts concerning demons and their habits emerge:
1. Demons seek to inhabit human beings, and when cast out immediately seek another human abode, or try to re-enter the one from whom they were cast out.

2. They will not willingly leave a human body. Demons do not cast each other out, but invite other demons to join them in their habitation (Lk. 11:14-18,26).
3. Only the power of God can cast out demons. When a ministry manifests this power, it is an attestation to its genuineness (Matt. 12:25-28).
4. In casting out demons, faith should be exercised against their attempts to re-enter the body they left or to enter others nearby. In the case of the deaf and mute child, Christ not only cast out the demon, but commanded it to "enter him no more!" (Mk. 9:25).
5. The power of God can cast out a demon, as well as bind and send it into the pit. Yet there is little record in the Scriptures that Jesus actually did so. On the other hand, He warned that a demon, when it was cast out, immediately sought to enter another body. Failing in this, the demon took other demons more wicked than itself, and made an attempt to return into the body out of which it had been cast. Jesus showed that this attempt by demons might be successful if the individual fails to obey God, and the Spirit of the Lord does not dwell in him.

Revelation 9:1-11 indicates that a great multitude of demons have in some previous time been bound and cast into the bottomless pit. However, the circumstances and time in which this happened is not clear. Matthew 8:29 seems to indicate that demons are free to continue their activities during this age, and for this reason they protested against Jesus sending them into the "abyss." Christ agreed to their request and permitted them to go into the herd of swine.

Chapter Twenty-Three

The Ministry of Casting Out Demons

The subject of casting out demons is much more complicated than one might suppose. There are many kinds of demons and many stages of demon oppression and possession. The responsibility of the person possessed for his condition also clearly enters into the picture. Moreover, one who is delivered and allows the demon to return bears a fearful responsibility. Strange as it may seem, some persons do not wish to have these spirits cast out of them. Mediums, clairvoyants, those given to fortunetelling, those dallying in ESP and psychic experimentation, all of whom know little about the Scriptures and its warnings, generally are under the delusion that they have a gift of God. And they do not wish to be told that they are harboring familiar spirits which belong to Satan's kingdom.

I have met persons who have consorted with these spirits over the years. In some cases they discover, often too late, the debilitating and erosive effect of these psychic powers upon their personality. Such individuals may find they have a fearful battle to get rid of them. As we have seen, occasionally a spiritist medium becomes alerted to the true nature of the spirits, and then endures a most agonizing and often prolonged battle to get rid of them. Once familiar spirits take possession of a person, they are exceedingly reluctant to leave.

The majority of people, fortunately, never get involved in psychic adventures. Still, all unsaved persons are oppressed to some extent by the enemy. Indeed, spirits often tempt people to commit deeds that they are heartily ashamed of afterward. Even Christians as a rule do not understand all they should about these malevolent forces that seek their destruction. It is the responsibility of everyone who names the Name of Christ to witness to others of Christ's power to save and that through repentance they can be set free from the powers of evil. Actually, repentance and faith in Christ delivers more people from the power of the devil than anything else.

> In humility correcting those who are in opposition, if God perhaps will grant them repentance, so that they may know the truth, and *that* they may come to their senses *and escape* the snare of the devil, having been taken captive by him to *do* his will (II Tim. 2:25,26).

King Saul, when first afflicted by an evil spirit, was delivered when David sang and played his harp in his presence. Surely many people who have been blinded by the enemy have been released from his power and brought to the Lord during a God-anointed song service, followed by the preaching of the Word.

There are certain kinds of spirits which are more easily cast out than others, including deaf spirits and blind spirits. Deliverance of deaf mutes in a meeting is usually very impressive to a congregation. Unfortunately, after the deaf person is delivered, he must be taught to speak just like a newborn babe. Since such individuals usually do not have trained personnel to help them during the critical period that follows, too often they lapse back into their old condition.

People classified by physicians as neurotics as a rule are oppressed by evil spirits. Their condition may have been brought on by self-will, lack of self-discipline, heavy indulgence in alcohol, or emotions such as envy, jealousy and uncontrolled temper. For the person to be permanently delivered, he must be willing to turn from the works of the flesh with all his heart.

Devils Cast Out in the Name of Jesus

It is important to observe that devils can be cast out only in and through the Name of Jesus. Believers have dominion over evil spirits, not through their own power, but through and by the authority of His Name. That's why the Seventy rejoiced, saying, "Lord, even the demons are subject to us in Your name" (Lk. 10:17).

Only those who have truly believed have this power. Believing means more than an intellectual conviction; it means believing Christ's words to the extent that we obey His commandments. "But why do you call Me 'Lord, Lord,' and not do the things which I say?" (Lk. 6:46). The power to cast out devils involves more than a casual belief in God's power to perform miracles.

Casting Out of Demons Requires More Than Magic

In the ministry of Paul, certain sons of Sceva witnessed the unusual power. For instance, when handkerchiefs were taken from Paul's body and placed on the sick, demons were cast out. Impressed by the methods that Paul was using, these vagabond exorcists decided to do likewise. They foolishly assumed that Paul's power lay in some kind of black magic similar to that which they used, only more potent. Carefully imitating the words and phrases that Paul used, they spoke to the spirit in a demon-possessed man: "We exorcise you by the Jesus whom Paul preaches" (Acts 19:13). The evil spirit at once saw that the exorcists were merely parroting words and did not have the power of Christ in their lives. The scene that followed was of a comic-opera nature.

> The evil spirit answered and said, "Jesus I know, and Paul I know; but who are you?" Then the man in whom the evil spirit was leaped on them, overpowered them, and prevailed against them, so that they fled out of that house naked and wounded (Acts 19:15,16).

All believers have the privilege of casting out demons. Jesus said, "These signs will follow those who believe: In My name they will cast out demons" (Mk. 16:17). But there is a definite anointing for this ministry. We need people who can challenge the evil powers. However, there is a price to pay, as is suggested in the words of Jesus regarding the epileptic demon: "This kind does not go out except by prayer and fasting" (Matt. 17:21).

In relating how he came into deliverance ministry, Dr. John G. Lake tells about an incident which occurred shortly before he went to Africa:

> At the close of the service a gentleman came to me, and pointing to a large red-letter motto on the wall, which read, "In my name they shall cast out devils," he said: "Do you believe that?" I replied, "I do." He said, "Do not answer hastily, for I have gone around the land seeking for a minister who would tell me he believed that. Many said that they did, but when I questioned them I found they wanted to qualify the statement." I said, "Brother, so far as I know my soul, I believe it with all my heart."
>
> Then he said, "I will tell you why I asked. Two and one-half years ago my brother who was a manager of a large grain elevator suddenly became violently insane. He was committed to the asylum, and is there today. Somehow he became possessed of an evil spirit. Physicians who have examined him declare that every function of his body and brain are apparently normal, and they cannot account for his insanity." I replied, "Brother, bring him on."
>
> On Sunday in the midst of the service, the man came, attended by the brother, the mother and an attendant of the institution.
>
> I stopped preaching, selected a half dozen persons whom I knew were people who had faith in God to join me in prayer for his deliverance. I stepped from the platform,

laid my hands on his head, and in the Name of Jesus Christ, the Son of God, commanded the devil that possessed him to come out of him. The Spirit of God went through my being like a flash of lightning. I knew in my soul that the evil spirit was cast out, and was not surprised when in a moment the man raised his head and spoke intelligently to me. A few days later he was discharged from the institution, returned home a healed man and resumed his former position as manager of a grain elevator. *(Excerpted from "The John G. Lake Sermons on Dominion Over Demons, Disease and Death.")*

Prayer and Fasting Needed to Cast Out Powerful Spirits

Some demons are more stubborn than others and can only be dislodged by special means. This proved to be the case in the epileptic boy whom the apostles could not heal. Emboldened by past successes, the apostles laid hands on him and rebuked the evil spirit, confidently expecting deliverance to come. To their surprise and consternation, not only did the demon stubbornly refuse to go, it showed its defiance by hurling the lad to the ground. If anything, it appeared that the lad was worse off than he was before.

The disciples may have supposed that there was something in the will of God that made healing the lad impossible. But Jesus quickly healed the child, showing that the cause of failure was because they did not have enough faith. To their question as to why they could not cast out this demon, Jesus replied:

> Because of your unbelief; for assuredly, I say to you, if you have faith as a mustard seed, you will say to this mountain, "Move from here to there," and it will move; and nothing will be impossible for you (Matt. 17:20).

Prayer and fasting is one of the means God has provided to strengthen faith for casting out demons, especially for difficult cases. Fasting can be used when all other means fail. The most difficult battles may be won through prayer and fasting. Why did the demon go when Jesus ministered to the child? Because Jesus Himself had fasted until the power of the Spirit rested upon Him. Jesus showed that, though some demons are more stubborn than others, all must go before those who have sufficient faith.

Binding the Demon

One thing should not be overlooked in this miracle. When the demon left, Christ expressly forbade it to ever return. He said, "Enter him no more!" (Mk. 9:25). Since Christ never spoke without a reason, it is evident that there are times when a demon should be bound so that it cannot return to the person. Experience indicates that many people who are delivered from a satanic possession often suffer a recurrence of their trouble simply because the demon powers are not bound. Christ said, "Whatever you bind on earth will be bound in heaven, and whatever you loose on earth will be loosed in heaven" (Matt. 18:18).

Can Demons be Cast Into the Pit?

It has sometimes been asked why, with the casting out of evil spirits, the demons are not bound and cast into the pit. It is perhaps true that demons may be bound for a period of time, but whether they can be indiscriminately sent into the pit cannot be certainly ascertained. Jesus commanded one demon to come out and to enter the person no more. Jesus took control of the demons that were cast out, and they could do nothing except what He told them to do. However, when the demons of a wild man protested against being sent into the deep (or the pit), declaring that the time of their punishment had not yet come, He allowed them to enter into the swine (Lk. 8:31,32).

It would appear from the words of Jesus that demons ordinarily are left free to wander about until they find a body that they may enter, or they may even re-enter the one from which they were cast out:

When an unclean spirit goes out of a man, he goes

through dry places, seeking rest; and finding none, he says, "I will return to my house from which I came." And when he comes, he finds *it* swept and put in order. Then he goes and takes with *him* seven other spirits more wicked than himself, and they enter and dwell there; and the last *state* of that man is worse than the first (Lk. 11:24-26).

The words Jesus spoke about the binding and loosing power of a believer (Matt. 18:18), among other things, imply they have the power to loose a person bound by an evil spirit and if necessary to bind the demon.

When an evil spirit is cast out, Jesus said it goes into the desert looking for a place to rest. But when it doesn't find any, it decides to return to its former habitation. If it finds it swept and cleaned, it takes other demons and they all enter the person. Then he is worse off than he was before (Lk. 11:24-26).

Since it is the habit of demons to seek re-entrance to their previous habitation, should a demon be bound so that it cannot return? Jesus did in some instances, but not in every case. Now if Jesus did not always bind the spirits — and it appears that as a general rule He did not — then it is not scriptural to bind every evil spirit that is cast out.

In the case of the lunatic who lived in the cemetery (Mk. 5:1-20; Lk. 8:26-39), an interesting colloquy between the demons and Jesus throws some light on this subject. When Jesus approached the man, the leader of the demons "begged Him that He would not command them to go out into the abyss" (Lk. 8:31). That would indeed be binding the demons, for if they were incarcerated in the pit, they would be prevented from molesting another person.

Matthew's account casts still further light on the subject. Here they pled with Jesus that their time of incarceration had not yet come. "Have You come here to torment us before the time?" (Matt. 8:29). Apparently there was a particular amount of time given them to roam the earth, and this time had not yet expired.

From this we gather that in the casting out of demons, we may not indiscriminately bind them by casting them into the abyss. A certain period of freedom has been allotted to them, and we may not overstep this. Nevertheless, the demon must obey the man or woman of God who is exorcising it from an afflicted person. It is obligated to leave, and if it stubbornly refuses to go and makes unnecessary resistance, then it would seem it has violated the limits of its freedom and forfeited consideration.

While we have no record that Jesus cast any evil spirit into the abyss or that He ordinarily bound them when they left, there certainly were occasions when He did bind the demon from returning to its previous victim. Such was the case when He cast out the powerful epileptic spirit (Lk. 9:37-42). He not only commanded it to leave, but commanded that it should never again re-enter the lad (Mk. 9:25). Why did Jesus do so in that case when He did not at other times, and instead warned the victims to take care lest the evil spirit return? The answer is simple: This lad had been possessed of the epileptic spirit from childhood through no fault of his own. And though delivered, he had no knowledge of how to resist the spirit should it return. Under the circumstances, the compassionate thing was to bind the spirit so it could not return. And this Jesus did.

On the other hand, as in the case of adults, in many instances, the individual — through sin, neglect or playing with the occult — opens the way for the evil powers to take possession. An adult, after witnessing what evil spirits can do, should gratefully serve the Lord, thus procuring God's protection from the enemy. However, if a person chooses to indulge in the lusts of the flesh instead of living in the Spirit, he will have to suffer the consequences. In such cases, we have no scriptural right to bind the demons. Adults cannot be denied freedom of choice.

Casting Out a Multitude of Demons

In many instances, people are possessed by more than one demon. This is often the case when a person is contemplating suicide. A person must be under a fearful oppression when he is willing to take the irrevocable step of self-destruction.

Pastor Maxwell Whyte tells of an instance in which a man called him on the telephone and said, "Brother Whyte, if you can't do something for me, I'm going to commit suicide." Pastor Whyte bluntly informed him that he believed that he had become demon possessed. The man was desperate and agreed to come to the pastor's home. The pastor and his wife took the man down into the basement of their home. As they began to plead the blood of Jesus, the demons began to come out, crying with a loud voice. But some that remained began to rebel. Pastor Whyte continues the story:

> We sat him in a chair and again sang some blood choruses. I pleaded the blood strongly against the evil powers and then gave a loud command in Jesus' Name for the demons to come out. I was startled at the reaction! Instantly this man literally shot one foot into the air off his seat and came down again. The demons then began to come out, crying with a loud voice. Again the terrible flow of mucous; we soaked up dozens of handkerchiefs. Again and again we commanded those terrible suicide demons to come out, and they responded each time, taking from a few seconds to 15 minutes to obey.
>
> We fought them ruthlessly, using the blood of Jesus and the Name of Jesus! They poured out of him; finally, they started to rebel and refused to leave his body.
>
> They were talking demons! I had heard about them, but never thought I would hold conversations with evil spirits. However, God was showing me much of the kingdom of darkness. When commanded to come out, they said, "No, shurrup," and insulted the Name of the Lord. It occurred to me that if they spoke, they could tell me how many more demons were in the body. Then the thought came that the devil is a liar from the beginning, so what was the use of asking the devil to speak the truth?
>
> The Holy Spirit then showed me that if I believed the

Name of Jesus to be all-powerful, even a demon would have to tell the truth, if commanded to do so in Jesus' Name. After one hour of fighting those suicide demons, and having cast out dozens and dozens, I spoke to them, saying, "Tell me how many more demons are left in that body?" They replied, "No, we won't, shurrup." I insisted, and further commanded them, but they continued to rebel and told me to be quiet! I refused, and bluntly commanded them, in Jesus' Name, to tell the truth; then to my astonishment, the demon said as clearly as you can imagine, "Twenty." I marked them down as each one came out with loud vomitings. After five more had come out, I asked again. And, again the demons refused to tell, but ultimately by pressure, they did tell, "Fifteen." I marked down five more, and again asked; again came the same performance, again the demon said, "Ten." This was repeated at five. When we came down to the last one, I felt we would have a wonderful confirmation.

The last "King Demon" refused to tell, but again he was forced to admit that there were none left after him, and we fought him for twenty minutes. He then came out with a tremendous vomit. Our poor brother then threw back his head and spoke gloriously in other tongues! He was delivered! He was happy!

In cases of this kind, vomiting may accompany the exit of the demons. This, of course, is just a natural physical reaction. It is a mistake, however, to expect this to happen in every case. There are those who try to establish a pattern for exorcising demons. One must be led of the Spirit in these matters. A healing service could take a bizarre turn if everyone oppressed by the enemy sought deliverance through vomiting. Strange demonstrations do occur in some instances, after which the person finds himself delivered from the power of the enemy.

Chapter Twenty-Four

Christ Brings Deliverance to the Captives

With the coming of Christ, a new era dawned in the world. Christ was the promised Redeemer of the Old Testament (Job 19:25) Who was to come and redeem the human race from bondage. He would do what the Law could not do. And so at the very beginning of His ministry, while in the synagogue in His home town of Nazareth, Jesus proclaimed His message of deliverance.

> *The Spirit of the LORD is upon Me, because He has anointed Me to preach the gospel to the poor; He has sent Me to heal the brokenhearted, to proclaim liberty to the captives and recovery of sight to the blind, to set at liberty those who are oppressed; to proclaim the acceptable year of the LORD* (Lk. 4:18,19).

This deliverance of which Jesus spoke included the setting free of captives who were under the oppression of Satan and his evil spirits.

Leaving Nazareth, Jesus went immediately to Capernaum and proceeded to demonstrate the Gospel of deliverance that He preached. A man in the synagogue was possessed of an insane or unclean spirit. The demon at once recognized Christ and cried out to be left alone, fearing that Jesus had come to destroy it (Lk. 4:33,34). Jesus rebuked the devil and cast it out. This was the first case in which a demon had been cast out in the presence of a congregation, and naturally it amazed the people.

> Then they were all amazed and spoke among themselves, saying, "What a word this *is*! For with authority and power He commands the unclean spirits, and they come out" (Lk. 4:36).

Christ's Dominion Over Satan Was Anticipatory of the Cross

How did Christ secure the victory over Satan? It was His perfect obedience even unto the death of the Cross. It was at Calvary that Satan, the ruler of this world, was judged (Jn. 16:11). Jesus declared, "Now is the judgment of this world; now the ruler of this world will be cast out" (Jn. 12:31).

As the result of His victory over Satan in the wilderness and His anticipated final victory at Calvary, Christ commissioned His disciples to cast out devils:

> Heal the sick, cleanse the lepers, raise the dead, cast out demons. Freely you have received, freely give (Matt. 10:8).

To the Seventy, whom He gave the same command, He said:

> Behold, I give you the authority to trample on serpents and scorpions, and over all the power of the enemy, and nothing shall by any means hurt you (Lk. 10:19).

And after Christ's death and resurrection, He could, in the Great Commission, give power over devils to all believers:

> And these signs will follow those who believe: In My name they will cast out demons (Mk. 16:17).

SPECIAL NOTE: A free gift subscription to CHRIST FOR THE NATIONS magazine is available to those who write to Christ For The Nations, P.O. Box 769000, Dallas, TX 75376-9000. This magazine contains special feature stories of men of faith and includes prophetic articles on the latest world developments. Why not include the names of your friends? (Due to high mailing rates, this applies only to Canada and the U.S.)

FREDA LINDSAY —
A woman who believes faith is practical!

In *My Diary Secrets,* Freda recounts her courtship and marriage to Gordon Lindsay and their life of ministry. Together they founded Christ For The Nations, a missionary organization that reaches around the world, and its interdenominational Bible institute, which has trained more than 26,000. This is an unforgettable story of God's anointing on a couple who devoted their lives to His service.

In *Freda: The Widow Who Took Up the Mantle,* Freda continues her life's chronicle, sharing how God enabled her to carry on the ministry He had given them after Gordon's death.

Freda's latest book, *A Book of Miracles,* relates how God's promised provison has been faithfully provided over her 84 years of life.

The ABCs for Godly Living is not just for children — parents and grandparents will benefit, too, from its words of wisdom. It covers salvation, healing, love, discipline, the Holy Spirit and many other subjects.

CFN Books • P.O. Box 769000 • Dallas, TX 75376-9000
(214) 302-6276